GABRIEL GERMAIN

Translated by Richard Howard

Homer

Evergreen Profile Book 11

GROVE PRESS, INC. EVERGREEN BOOKS LTD.
NEW YORK LONDON

FIRST PUBLISHED IN THIS EDITION 1960. ALL RIGHTS RESERVED.

Library of Congress Catalog Card Number: 60-6215

Evergreen Profile Books are published

in the United States by Grove Press, Inc.

64 University Place   New York 3, N.Y.

in Great Britain by Evergreen Books Ltd.

20 New Bond Street   London, W. 1

Distributed in Canada by McClelland & Stewart Ltd., 25 Hollinger Road, Toronto 16

First published in France by Éditions du Seuil, Paris, as Homère

MANUFACTURED BY MOUTON & CO., IN THE NETHERLANDS

Homer
by Gabriel Germain

Contents

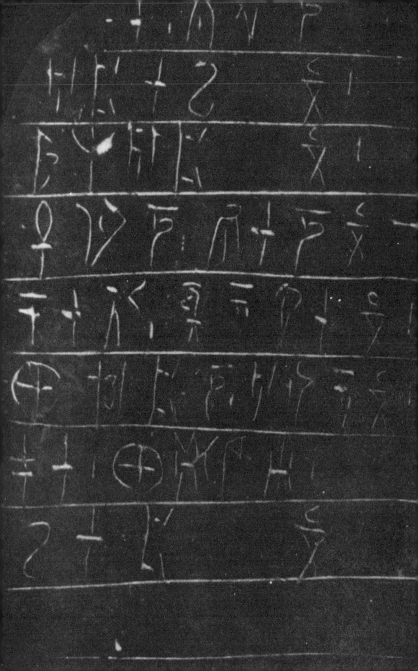

Tell me why you weep and lament deep in your heart,
Hearing the sufferings of the Greeks, and those of Ilion?
The gods have wrought them with their own hands, have spun the ruin
Of these men, so that for those to come, the Song remains.

Homer

HISTORICAL AND CHRONOLOGICAL FRAMEWORK

The Homeric epic describes, or is thought to describe, a world considerably anterior to the epic itself, when the Greeks, whom it calls Achaeans (or sometimes Danaians), occupied the Peloponnesus, central Greece, Thessaly, Crete, the Cyclades, and Rhodes. Agamemnon, their common leader in the struggle against Troy, was King of Mycenae and of Argos. This represented the highest point of Mycenaean civilization.

That civilization developed in and then around the Peloponnesus during the second millenium before the modern era. Its chronology is still in dispute. The following dates must be considered approximate.

Between 2000 and 1750 B.C., establishment of the Achaeans on the shores of the Mediterranean.

Seventeenth century B.C., first palaces of Mycenae and Tiryns.

1550-1400 B.C., extension of the Achaean influence through central Greece and as far as Rhodes.

1400-1300 B.C., high point of Mycenaean civilization, reaching as far as Crete. The Hittite archives give evidence of contact between the Hittite empire and a kingdom of Akhaiwa, whose site remains in dispute (1335-1300 B.C.). Achaeans on Cyprus.

In the course of a lengthy crisis starting in the thirteenth century B.C., the Mycenaean world succumbs to a second wave of Greek peoples, the Dorians (represented in the Hellenic tradition by Heracles and his descendants).

During this period, successive villages appear on the site presumed to be Troy; the one possibly corresponding to the Homeric Troy would be inhabited between 1365 and 1200 B.C. (according to Claude Schaeffer). The dates given by the Greek tradition for the Trojan War correspond, in our chronology, to 1193 or 1183 B.C. Obviously they must be put back about two hundred years if the war is to coincide with the period of Mycenaean civilization (1385 B.C., according to Jean Bérard).

As for the epic itself and the possible dates of *The Iliad* and *The Odyssey*, see below, chapter I, and the end of chapter III.

Gold mask, supposedly Agamemnon's, from one of the tombs of Mycenae

. . . One and the same wave the world over, the same wave since Troy
Rolls its haunch even to us. Upon the open sea far from us this
breath was printed once . . .
And the murmur one night was loud in the chambers:
death itself, to the sound of its conchs, could not be heard.

Saint-John Perse, *Seamarks*

SOME PATHS TOWARD THE SUMMIT

Homeric scholars can take pride in being the first of all western exegetes. Thanks to the Byzantines, their tradition has never been broken. In the Orient, only the Vedic commentators extend back further in a continuous line, and after them come those expounding the oldest parts of the Old Testament. In writing this book, I continue the line of that first teacher somewhere in Greece who made his students recite: *"Mênin aeïde, thea . . ."* [1] And some echoes of that voice reach me still.

Yet when I turn back to my purpose, which is to facilitate the reading of the Homeric *poems*, how intimidated I should feel were I one of those who need company for reassurance. Samuel Eliot Bassett, the American who more than twenty years ago wrote the only worthwhile book on Homer's poetry in more years than I care to reckon, says at its start: "The impression, created by the masters of Homeric studies in the nineteenth century, that the study of Homer from the point of view of poetry is not worthy of a scholar, still persists." [2]

His indictment reminds me of the defense of a thesis on Greek literature. A member of the jury said to the candidate: "The beginning of your study interested me, but it ended as a humanist's work!" The accent of reproach he put on those

9

last words echoed strangely in the Sorbonne which, after all, is no longer the Sorbonne of 1500. "A humanist's work!" – because the future doctor, "attired in candid honesty" if not in white linen, had thought it only fair to end his overlong analyses with a few pages of more properly literary appraisal.

I shall not take up the axe with which Péguy decimated the followers of the famous "method" which is so exhaustive that it prevents a truly scrupulous mind from ever finishing a piece of work. But I cannot help repeating his advice to the innocent reader, who simply wants to understand and enjoy his Homer: "Don't tell yourself: he's great. Don't tell yourself that. Don't tell yourself anything. Read the text. Don't tell yourself: this is Homer. This is the greatest. This is the first. This is the master. This is the father of all the rest . . . Read the text, and don't put anything between yourself and the text. Above all, no echoes, no memories . . . Read the text without any interference, without any preparation, without any ceremony. As if each of these *cantos*, these songs, these rhapsodies, were a new work that had just appeared from week to week, from month to month – as if it were the latest thing." [3]

And if I contradict myself for the moment by discussing briefly the interest and scope of the studies with which modern scholarship surrounds the Homeric epic, I do so, in the last analysis, only in order to improve our approach to the text itself.

The archeologist's trench

In the whole of secular literature, only Shakespeare and Dante have accumulated as much literary and symbolic com-

mentary as Homer. Cumulus clouds that thunder among themselves more often than they emit flashes that might illuminate anything else. Still, there they are; very much there.

It would probably take more than one lifetime to become well acquainted with all these texts, even if they could be found assembled somewhere. No Homeric scholar has ever made a total count. Confronted with the results of so much reverence, such loving vigils which, from century to century have been unremittingly heaped up around this unknown man or these unknown men whom we call Homer, we feel both moved and increasingly melancholy. For if we trace out the viewpoints offered by these innumerable studies, we soon see that they all converge on the epoch in question by two or three main avenues. The more frequently we pass back and forth along them, the more they become gigantic ruts where the learned ants trample each other, each tugging his straw behind him, without ever being able to break out. Zeus, of course, must be delighted by the spectacle from the heights of his Olympus, in that solitude of sullen contemplation Homer likes to attribute to him. But if those of us who run about at the bottom of the trench have not been granted from birth or acquired at school a crustacean's instincts, we are soon engulfed in a nightmare of mud.

First of all, there is the archeologist's trench. This was supposed to carry us far, not only to the places described in the epic, but even to the remains of its heroes. Schliemann, not content with having unearthed Troy at Hissarlik, believed

11

he had awakened Agamemnon in his tomb. We have retreated considerably since, and not only in the case of Agamemnon. The mound at Hissarlik, with its layered villages, offers considerable information as to the protohistory of the various peoples who settled on the shores of the Aegean, but it takes an overdeveloped imagination to squeeze a city of any importance into these meager measurements.[4] Worthy minds have offered strong arguments[5] against this identification ("imposed" by the Homeric text), which is in a fair way to becoming classical. It is no small paradox that certain passages of *The Iliad* nevertheless give the impression that their author knew the topography of the region personally;[6] we must conclude either that he set Troy there, but somewhere else besides Hissarlik; or that, confronted by a pre-established tradition, he was no more sensitive to its impossibilities than an enthusiastic excavator. Certainly, of the two, it is the poet who has every right to the free exercise of his imagination. But in this case, the findings of archeology fall wide of his text.

One main fact remains: The two epics refer us to a period which, thanks to the archeologists, has been recovered by history, that of the civilization we call Mycenaean because Mycenae and the cities of Agamemnon's kingdom are its best-known centers. The ruins of Mycenae and of Tiryns still bore witness to its vigor for the Hellenes, who attributed them to the Cyclops,[7] and they are no less striking to modern visitors. Behind the Mycenaean world lies Minoan Crete, which has unexpectedly confirmed certain details once regarded as legendary.

But it does not diminish the inestimable value of such a discovery to wonder what areas it illuminates in the Homeric text. In the enthusiasm which always accompanies the sudden exhumation of a mass of new materials, we are at first tempted to recognize in the hands of the epic characters the very objects we are in the process of digging up. Then, upon examination, doubt replaced some of the certitudes that had been adopted too quickly. Mrs. H. L. Lorimer, who has made the most recent summary of our information in this area, has not hesitated to admit as much: "Features of bronze age culture are doubtless exemplified in the Homeric poems, but they are much less considerable than was once supposed."[8]

It is not difficult to see as much for ourselves: the objects that have most readily provoked Mycenaean parallels are

14

luxury objects, pieces from the royal treasury such as Nestor's cup, the helmet given by Meriones to Ulysses, and the shield of Achilles, some of the figures on which recall those of the Minoans themselves.[9]

In this last case, the description of the dancing floor built at Knossos by Dedalus is connected, through Ariadne, with the Theseus legend, and thereby with the royal tradition of Athens. We shall retain such connections for later in the discussion. But we must immediately consider details of this nature on the scale of the two epics as a whole: their *poetic* dimension is insignificant. If the shield of Achilles, by virtue of the scenes represented on it, is weighty with significance, the technique and the origin of these figures is of no consequence whatever; their very multiplicity, moreover, converts them into a work which only the imagination of a great poet could conceive, and only the art of a god execute.

Obviously, it is not descriptions of works of art or of royal arms which constitute Homer's value for us. Yet it might have been thought that by dating these objects one could thereby date the passages where they occur, on the principle that Homer could not have seen them because, in his time, none of them was in circulation – even if we place him in the ninth century before the modern era. It was easy to reach the conclusion, in all such cases, that Homer belonged to a poetic tradition anterior to the collapse of Mycenaean civilization. Thus Mrs. Lorimer, apropos of Ulysses' helmet, observing that it is made of cloth or leather (the material to which are attached the boar's teeth that are its peculiarity) and that it therefore could not have survived through the ages, concludes: "Its image can have been preserved only in the amber of traditional poetry, transmitted with an astonishing verbal fidelity."[10] This question brings us to a problem of poetic interest: the remote origins of the epic.

If only for this reason, it is worth taking the trouble to stop for a moment and consider this line of reasoning. But what confronts us? A matter of handing down this helmet some five or six centuries. Yet what cathedral crypt cannot show some sacerdotal vestment, a miter, an altarcloth dating from the fourteenth or fifteenth century? Why, similarly, could not some great family (not to mention the temples) preserve a Mycenaean object, taking it along on its Ionian migrations? But above all, why consider only the perishable object itself,

17

Mycenae: burial ground of the original palace

when images of it existed on solid enough materials: vases, seals, small ivory reliefs which Mrs. Lorimer meticulously itemizes? Since the publication of her book, several ivory tablets, unearthed at Mycenae in 1953, have been added to this collection. These recovered figures were probably buried in Homer's time, but the more they multiply, the more chances there are that others circulated them, readily crossing seas and centuries.

Let us forget details at thus point. It remains true that the written documents of the classical Orient entitle us to believe that a state of Akhaiwa existed among the neighbors of the Hittite empire. Even if we may hesitate over the precise center of its power, even if we are not certain that we recognize the familiar names of the epic in the Hittite transcriptions, it is enough to know that the royalty of Agamemnon is not all epic myth. Then, the discovery on the supposed site of Pylos, old Nestor's capital, of important archives (purely administrative, unfortunately), followed by a sufficiently advanced deciphering to give us an idea of their contents, as well as that of other tablets of the same sort previously found at Knossos and recently at Mycenae, indicate that organized monarchies existed in the Peloponnesus and Achaean Crete.[11] They had their scribes and therefore – they too – their bureaucracy. Division of labor was quite advanced. The language, so far as we can judge, offered few major differences from that of Homer. We can recognize the names of the most important Greek divinities: Zeus, Hera, Poseidon, Athena, probably even Dionysos, to the astonishment of many scholars who thought the latter of more recent date. Among the names of individuals, 58 are found in the epic. That of Nestor is still missing (one of the pranks of chance); those of Achilles and Hector are attributed to obscure persons.

This sheds considerable light on the Achaean world; and, to a certain degree, the epic benefits by it. But there is also the other side – the shadow side. It is enough to have read *The Iliad* as a diligent amateur to know that the Achaean kings, and Agamemnon first of all, do not have the style of monarchs whose power is based on organized states. They rule like caids in the Berber mountains: among equals, there are tempestuous discussions, even outright disputes; between lesser men, cudgel or sword. Where are their scribes? Where are their archives? *The Iliad* mentions writing only once, in the vague form of a

19

group of "signs," and this in the legend of Bellerophon, which constitutes a digression. Everything occurs as if their great expedition were led without preconceived plan; only the supply service seems to be organized, unless the credit for this belongs to the commercial instincts of the neighboring peoples.[12] So that at the very moment when linguistic and religious tradition apparently tightens the links between Homer and the Mycenean era, we understand better, parallel with this *rapprochement*, how alien the poet is to certain essential characteristics of this society.

We can add to this striking example other wide divergences of usage which have long been a matter of common knowledge: the author of *The Iliad* describes Troy as a city which possesses real temples (not chapels in great houses) and in these temples real statues; he is also unaware of the characteristic use made of mural paintings in palaces, and he attributes cremation to a people who buried their dead. Not only that: one can also wonder if certain facts regarded as a Mycenaean heritage do not derive from more recent sources. One must consider, on the one hand, regional survivals; thus Lesbos, with the Penthilides who claimed descent from Agamemnon through Orestes, maintained a monarchy of the Homeric type until the seventh century B.C.[13] Chariots were still used in Euboea by the combatants of the Lelantine war in this same century. The Greeks

Detail of the geometric amphora of the Dipylon (National Museum of Athens)

of Asia saw them in action among their neighbors the Lydians,[14] and the colonists of Cyrenaica found them in use among the Africans.[15] We must also remember that court usage is virtually analogous everywhere: the throne and the scepter are no more Mycenaean than oriental, and it is the ancient Orient which furnishes us with the equivalents of the titles of respect the Homeric characters use toward each other.[16] In the absence of literary documents anterior to Homer among the Greeks, who is to decide, in many such cases of detail, if the poet is benefiting from a tradition of his own race or if he is imagining the realities of the past according to what he sees around him?

What the linguists have to say

The educated public may be aware of the contributions of archeology, but it takes less account of the enormous labor performed upon Homer by the linguists. Ruins, objects in museums can be touched and seen, while vocabularies and linguistic classifications are incomprehensible without a previous initiation. Yet the importance of the results achieved should not be overlooked. Thanks to the comparative study of Indo-European languages, to a knowledge of Greek dialects which the science of inscriptions extends beyond literary texts or fills out in their absence, we have been able to achieve increasing clarity about the structure of the composite language Homer used. The deciphering of the Mycenaean tablets will probably involve a shift in certain details; but the essential points remain fixed. It is indeed unfortunate that their full value cannot be demonstrated without minute and technical explanations which would be out of place here, for to understand the *poetic effect* produced in Greek by Homer's language, this philological basis is indispensable.

What characterizes this Homeric Greek in relation to the so-called classical language of the great Athenian authors is not only a certain degree of archaism – such as separates the *Chanson de Roland* from a tragedy by Racine, for instance. As a matter of fact, this comparison would be weak on both sides: first, Homer possesses a vocabulary which permits the analysis of thought and sentiment, the expression of sensation, with more abundance and subtlety than that of Turold, which makes him more "modern" than the author of the *chanson de geste*; and second, what separates him from classical Attic is not merely a matter of less developed phonetics, of still un-unified grammatical forms – rather superficial differences which would not hamper our own students for long. The true difference is that Attic is a coherent whole, insofar as the real dialect of a well-defined collectivity can be, while the Homeric language mixes various ways of speaking with its Ionian base and draws from this inexhaustible reservoir the forms of words which the verse requirements impose. As a matter of fact, if Homer is actually obliged *not* to abide by his natal way of speaking, it is because he is a prisoner of a verse form, the dactylic hexameter, which does not correspond to the natural rhythm of the Greek language. The latter naturally tends to the iambic.[17]

We encounter here a fact which has no equivalent in our own poetic history. The Greek verses based on the iamb and the trochee (that is, feet comprising a short and a long syllable variously placed) find their approximate equivalents in the metric of ancient India.[18] They are, therefore, like the Hellenic language, of Indo-European stock. This is not the case with the hexameter (formed of six feet, of which the last is obligatorily composed of two long syllables, and whose other five feet can be constituted of either a long syllable followed by two shorts or of two longs). The hexameter doubtless comes out of the Aegean world, where the Greeks received it from an earlier civilization, but this is all we can say. Yet the Greek language is so constituted that its words often present too many or not enough short syllables together, a difficulty avoided by a series of professional tricks, actually quite easy to acquire, which permit the poet to extend or duplicate short syllables and shorten long ones.

Why have the epic poets undertaken these perpetual acrobatics, instead of choosing another verse form? The answer is to be looked for in religious experience. Greek tradition attributes the genesis of this kind of verse to the prophetic sanctuaries, and in fact, as long as the oracles were in the form of poetry, they were generally given in hexameters. Hexameter was also used in the great religious festivals to narrate the sacred legends of the local deity. By attributing to Homer a collection of such hymns, the oldest of them not remote from the Homeric period, tradition has maintained a sense of the original links between sacred and epic poems. Nevertheless the epic represents the bards as court poets, not as cantors attached to temples; obviously we must not go too far afield in our search for links between Homer and the sacerdotal milieu – which for the Greeks, moreover, did not constitute a caste comparable to that of the Brahmans or the Druids.[19]

In any case, the epic language was distinguished from the ordinary way of speaking by archaisms of vocabulary and by a mixture of dialects not at all surprising in regions of mixed populations. Even the most ordinary words could be transformed in order to accommodate them to the hexameter. The infinitive of the verb to be (what word could be more ordinary?) could appear either in its everyday form, eïnaï, or in two Eolian forms, emmen and emmenaï; the latter in turn could lose one of their m's if necessary. Thus, because of language alone, no English translation can give a precise equivalent of the Homeric text. Of course a nimble mind could amuse itself by finding or inventing equivalents, archaisms, and variants. But it would be a waste of time: the result would seem merely eccentric. We who have never had a poetic language separated from our ordinary speech, who cannot even resort, like our ancestors, to a "style noble" – we must make a considerable effort to imagine the luster, tinged with the sacred, which its hearers discerned in the Homeric language simply as language.

We must similarly try to conceive of a second quality which derives from the very structure of the ancient verse line. It

23

Fragment of the tablets of a cook of Knossos, deciphered by Ventris

could contain flat stretches and obvious fillers, but it never *sounded* like prose. With its six strong beats, the succession of its long and short syllables, its caesura (slightly variable), its secondary rests, whether it was supported, as at its origin, by the sound of the cithara (of which we know nothing), or whether it was merely declaimed, the hexameter, whatever its subject, always remained on the level of poetry.[20] This is what made possible the long narrative in verse, which has become so easily intolerable to us. I do not mean that the ancient hexameter guaranteed against any decline in poetic intensity – as we know from the ancients themselves – but that this intensity never diminished to a point where the current absolutely ceased to flow.

This continuous texture of the poem, its nature still musical, or quasi-musical, is one we can scarcely feel today. If we only knew how the ancients publicly declaimed poetry or recited it to themselves! But we are without precise information. Perhaps, at least, we can imagine it from the Vedic recitations still practiced in India and which, because of the sacred character of the texts, have certainly been kept as near their origins as possible. Here is how one reliable witness [21] describes them: "Stressed with clockwork precision, the strophes are reeled off, the voice falling slightly at the half-pause, a little more distinctly at the pause. Slight movements of the fingers, sometimes curled over the thumbs, sometimes stretched out, mark the nuances of tone. The latter assumes a refined inflection in the passages of melopoeia, which is elsewhere marked by the strict alternation of long and short syllables. It is something very mannered, very scholarly, though apparently simple."

Such a diction, of course, like that of Arabic poetry – essentially rhythmic – excludes all expressiveness of an affective nature, which we strive for.[22] It is a question of remaining faithful to the *music of the verse* (the term is genuinely appropriate here), and not to sentiment. The wide use Homer makes of accessory pauses and run-on lines [23] is probably an attempt to compensate for this primary indifference to emotion.

Insofar as it permits us to inventory the poet's resources, linguistics actually helps us penetrate the secrets of his labor. On the other hand, little credit can be given to its attempts to bridge historical gaps and link the two poems together from this or that conjectural origin. The etymology of the proper names of the characters and the place-names is an extremely delicate science when history itself does not establish guide lines for hypotheses. One cannot construct systems upon it.[24] There is more future in the study which, by comparing the most ancient Indo-European languages, attempts to recover the physiological, psychological, and cosmological notions implied by certain terms that occur frequently in the Homeric poems.[25] It is a kind of cross-section through the linguistic terrain which makes possible the exhumation of various archaic levels of thought. All the same, in this "ideological" archeology as in the other, one can no more credit the poet with a precise awareness of the primitive meaning of his language than with a knowledge of cities already buried in his own time. We must use the results it furnishes with critical prudence.

It is within the confines of linguistics and a science of poetic facts (which has still to be organized) that the studies of the Homeric "formulas" are located. They deal not only with the familiar characterizations of each hero; there exist many other elements in the epic which are repeatedly made use of in the same way: entire lines or hemistichs which recur when analogous circumstances call for the same actions, the same ceremonies, the same invocations. In *The Iliad*, 5,605 such lines (out of approximately 16,000) have been counted, either altogether or partly repetition, and 3,648 in *The Odyssey* (out of some 10,000). The conclusion has been drawn correctly that "a single poet could never have created this entire series of formulas." [26] Others, then, had to prepare the way for Homer. As another consequence, he did not seek originality of expression: "For him, as for all the bards, to versify was to remember." [27] Scholars have vied happily with each other in estimating how many centuries of epic poetry it must have taken to perfect the art of "formulary verse" – precisely the centuries needed to fill the gap between Mycenaean civilization and Homer's period.

We must look closer. Not all the Homeric formulas can be considered on the same level. The religious origin of some is evident, and in this case, the memory of the priests and the faithful suffices to assure their transmission, as does the tradition of the oracles and the hymns. Others, which relate to manners, perhaps merely accommodate to verse real functions or titles, and create others to imitate them. In this case, it is the memory of courts and chancelleries that is at work. There are, on the other hand, formulas "to fill up gaps," often of considerable extent. Thanks to them, poets who where supposed to improvise, that is, who relied on both their memory and their verbal skill, were never in danger of not "filling out" a line. It is these latter which presuppose the existence of professional bards, but there is absolutely no reason why they must be counted by generations.

Any flowering of a literary genre involves, by the mere phenomenon of imitation, even scarcely conscious imitation, the swift creation of language habits, and the latter necessarily turn into formulas when metrics imposes constraints on expression. Any student of the French classical theater knows to what degree it too utilizes "formulas," all the more frequent as the authors in question are productive and hard-pressed. Every successful author quickly develops his conventions, his stereotypes. Students have been able to attribute an anonymous tragedy, *La Mort de Solon*, to Corneille principally because of certain Corneillan "formulary" lines; [28] but (and this is the

26

argument's weak point) such self-borrowings and repetitions were not unusual at the time, even in the prose of Moliere's *Don Juan*.[29]. Racine in turn hold's sway, and he is quickly followed by Campistron, where we find frequent borrowing from the earlier author.

Naturally the profusion of formulas is not as great in the French classical theater as in Homer; but the alexandrine is not the hexameter, and above all, the concern to escape accusations of plagiarism imposed limits on the seventeenth-century author. But when an author made borrowings from his own works he had fewer scruples, and there exists an entire book devoted to Corneille as an imitator of himself.[30] Similarly, it is wise to recognize that a Homeric *ritornello* can be the poet's own invention as well as a unique expression. We know that *The Iliad* and *The Odyssey*, if they possess certain formulas in common, have also formulas of their own which they do not share with each other. And the fact that an Athenian orator offers, as Homeric and formulary, an expression not to be found in either of the two poems proves that secondary authors, working in Homer's wake, did not refrain from creations of this type.[31] Besides, what reasons would one have for denying the author or authors of *The Iliad* and *The Odyssey* the faculty and the taste for minting a large share of their formulas, since we must finally attribute the paternity of the genre to someone and find a moment when "to versify" was something else besides "to remember"? [32]

The scandal of creation

Rather, it is all too clear why, since Wolf, scholars have tried to weaken the scandal of epic creation by diluting it in a long brew of insipid centuries. All creation is scandalous – at least for minds which, in their eagerness to preserve an appearance of order and calm at all costs, attempt to schematize a closed world where effects never exceed causes – a view, moreover, which is justifiable and necessary within certain limits and for certain purposes. It was therefore inevitable that after having put God in a cage – and lost the cage – the *Philosophes* of the Age of Enlightenment should also want to wring the necks of poets: trifling spoil-sports, but they made the mistake of appearing at all-too-significant points in the human past to be altogether overlooked. There remained the recourse of denying them any original faculties, and therefore making their works into a simple *summa* of a multitude of tiny inventions (so tiny that the creative spark was no longer noticeable) produced over a great number of years by a multitude of anonymous poets (so vague that no one would dare pronounce on their behalf that annoying word *genius*).

This is why so many scholars who have perhaps never defined the metaphysics of their principles (though there is no worse sickness than a masked metaphysic), though now less inclined to make the Homeric poems into a Harlequin's mantle sewn by the rhapsodes' needle [33] out of *lays* from the popular imagination, continue to refer the tradition of the Homeric bards back to the Mycenaean period. Yet there are two equally evident propositions:

1) The Mycenaeans certainly had poets, for there is no

Geometric vase of the Dipylon (National Museum of Athens)

society, however "primitive" and wretched, which does not possess some kind of poetry.

2) Unfortunately we know absolutely nothing about them. It would be not only an arbitrary act to apply to them the image of the bard furnished by the Homeric epic, it would be a dreadful sophism, for we would thereby take as solved precisely what is in question.

There remains open for conjecture only the always inadequate route of historical analogies. These tell us that around this same Mediterranean, through the centuries, brilliant civilizations have left no epics behind them, even when they were (like the Cananeans of Ras Shamra) given to writing mythological poems. In Israel, in Egypt, the subject of minor epic compositions is probably drowned in chronicles, that is, in royal inscriptions; but after all, it is we who imagine we recognize an epic subject in the tone of the narrative, whereas we are probably establishing a distinction between history and fiction that is perhaps too clear-cut for Oriental minds. Arabo-Berber Africa, which has prolonged so many ancient usages to our own day, has not left a single line of epic, even after the great adventures of the Almoravides and the Almohades. What Berber society has to say about its strong men has never extended beyond the lament, and it is difficult to find any of these which go back more than two generations. All these peoples, however, have had lyric poetry and professional poets. We may counter this absence by the epic chants of the southern Slavs, but it is no slur on the merits of the latter to emphasize the distance separating these limited works from the enormous artistic compositions of the Greek epic.

Consider French literature. Despite tremendous efforts, no one has ever discovered proof of a long period of poetic preparation which might "explain" the flowering of the *chansons de geste*, which might conceal, frankly, the scandal of the *Chanson de Roland*. At the end of a fiery study,[34] Italo Siciliano concludes: "The *chansons de geste* are precise, *organized*, complex poetic phenomena, the product of a synthesis of old elements – inert and indefinable – and of new, creative elements: and they do not have, they cannot have, any other date than that at which this synthesis occurred in the mind and art of the poet." Similarly, Homer finds heroic legends, traditions of royal families and sanctuaries, old Oriental myths, sometimes fallen to the level of folklore and fairy tale. We are not denying the fact that legends of heroes, in particular, had already given rise to these poems. Their style cannot have reached the degree of sureness it has without previous attempts, and a share of these attempts will have derived from profane, if the remainder must have been devoted to religious, poetry. But to find in this scattered material a sufficient explanation of the work as we know it is to confuse the mongrel with the thoroughbred.

Let us avoid another source of confusion. The Homeric legends of heroes are generally connected with cities whose brilliance was particularly great in the Mycenaean period. To this degree they can be called Mycenaean, but to this degree only. It would be rash to conclude that these legends therefore took the forms they have in Homer. Actually, this would be contrary to the nature of legends, which is to become richer until the moment people lose interest in them. Consider the battle of Roncevaux seen by Eginhard, and what it becomes with Turold!

One remark in conclusion. The Pylos script, which does not permit us to distinguish the prosodic quantity of the vowels, which furnishes few diphthongs, which does not represent double consonants, which does not indicate the final *l, m, n, r,* or *s,* is quite inadequate to transcribe a line of Greek verse. Classical script, on the contrary, seems so well adapted to its notation that the notion has been advanced that it was actually invented to serve poetry.[35] That that script, at least, might have favored the construction of long, essentially artistic epics, is

"These men who sing at feasts do not want
to be taken for ordinary hired entertainers . . ."

also an argument against disproportionately extending the period preparatory to the Homeric works. The oldest alphabetical inscriptions are not dated earlier than around 800 B.C.; if we agree that there is little chance of having unearthed the very first such evidences, and that we must therefore go back some years before to reach the origins, we will perhaps not be far from the origins, too, of the epic invention itself.

The bards

It is true, then, that we cannot consider the Homeric epic as a work without antecedents, as the first expression of the Hellenic soul, but it would be just as dangerous to regard it as the setting sun of a long epic day – a day lasting several centuries. The masterpieces of a genre never wait until its conclusion to appear. They are more often closer to its beginnings than to the middle of its history. Who, on the tragic stage, will surpass Aeschylus? What comic writer will equal Aristophanes? What historian preserves Thucidydes' surgical profundity? Have the French ever produced an epic even the equal of the *Chanson de Roland*? It is Péguy who says of the literary creator: "At the same time that he takes on *métier* and habit (that corset), he also takes on age, he gains by aging, he acquires by aging, he wins by losing. He loses freshness, he loses the primal innocence, that unique, irreplaceable value." [36] One can find traces of the aging of the genre in *The Odyssey*; it would be much more difficult to indicate them in *The Iliad*: its age is the full brilliance of young maturity.

The authors of the *chansons de geste* occasionally do not scorn the authority of a ghostly Ancient who will lend a certain prestige to their theme. *Roland* mentions "*Virgilie e Omer*"; [37] it is apparent that the author is not too sure who these noble old men are, but at least their names are there. The bards, as the author of *The Odyssey* presents them, – and he must have known them better than we – boast of having no masters and of owing everything to divine inspiration. I shall let them speak for themselves at the end of this chapter, but first I want to indicate two points. These men who sing at banquets and in places of pilgrimage do not want to be considered only hired entertainers; they are conscious of their dignity, proud of their profession. This is certainly one of the reasons that lead them to cry that they are inspired. But in

32

their cry they reveal the amazement, the wonder which seizes the truly *honest* mind confronted with the mystery of creation, with this voice within us which says better than we ourselves what we have dreamed (and what we have not dreamed) of saying. And since anything unforeseen passed in their time for a divine manifestation, they gave first credit for their gift to the gods – which does not keep them from being, at the same time, quite satisfied with their work. I doubt whether this would be the state of mind of men for whom "to versify" would be "to remember" and nothing more.

Men of a *métier*, certainly, possessing all its tricks and traditions. It is a great security for an artist to be able to rest on a tradition; it is a reservoir of strength; he need not exhaust his gifts by producing everything within himself. Among such men comes a profound thinker who takes everything offered to him and makes it his own. He casts upon the world that gaze of genius which grasps the sensuous and the invisible in the same foreshortening. He invents, or he makes a success of the first great *constructed* poem. Thus *The Iliad* is born.

How lucky we are! Of Homer as a man, the Greek tradition itself knew nothing *historical*. Only his name, which is, moreover, "rather singular." [38] The confusion this tradition admits on a point as simple as his birthplace is sufficient evidence that it has not been able to assemble any of those "anecdotes," commentary on which, incessantly developed by the *concierges* of scholarship, dispenses, in the case of modern writers, with their proceeding to the essential questions. It is impossible to discover, or to suppose, some petty failing that would permit us to despise Homer. It is impossible to reach him except through his work. We must confront him in his greatness.

In heroic times: the grand seigneur poet

*Nestor and Ulysses go to Achilles in the name of the Achaian
leaders. It is night:*

and they found Achilleus delighting his heart in a lyre, clear-
[sounding,
splendid and carefully wrought, with a bridge of silver upon it,
which he won out of the spoils when he ruined Eëtion's city.
With this he was pleasuring his heart, and singing of men's fame,
as Patroklos was sitting over against him, alone, in silence.

The Iliad, ix *

The bard and reality

In Ithaca, in the palace, before Ulysses' return:

To that audience the great singer still sang: and they sat round,
hanging on the song which told of the woeful return entailed by
Pallas Athene upon such Greeks as had gone to Troy. In her
upper storey, Penelope, that most circumspect daughter of Icarius,

---

caught rising snatches of the minstrelsy. Her wit pieced these together into their sense. Down she came by the high stairs from her quarters and entered the great hall: not indeed alone, for always two waiting women closely followed her. So, like a stately goddess among mortals, she descended upon the suitors: to halt there where the first great pillar propped the massy roof. As veil for her face she held up a fold of her soft wimple: and the ever watchful maidens covered her, one on either side. Thus stood she and wept, till she found words to address the inspired bard.

"Phemius," she cried, "do you not know many other charmed songs for people's ears? Songs in which poets have extolled the great deeds of Gods or men? Sing one of those, here from your place in the company which will, none the less, sit silently drinking and listening. But this lamentable tale give over: the sorrow of it slowly melts my heart within my bosom; for you tell of the event which has brought down upon me – me above all women – this unappeasable pain. So continually does my memory yearn after that dear head. O my lost hero! whose glory had spread throughout Hellas and Argos, the very heart of the land!"

Telemachus decently cut her short. "My Mother, why take it amiss that our trusty singer should entertain us as the spirit moves him? I think it is not poets who bring things to pass, but rather Zeus who pays out to men, the Makers, their fates at his whim: we have no cause against Phemius for drawing music out of the hard fate of the Danaans. A crowd ever extols the song which sounds freshest in its ears. Harden your heart and mind to hear this tale."

The Odyssey, i *

* All quotations from *The Odyssey,* translated by T. E. Shaw, © 1932 by Bruce Rogers, are reprinted by permission of Oxford University Press, Inc., New York.

Rhapsode of the fifth century B.C. (British Museum)

The inspired singer in all his glory

In the palace of Alcinous, king of the Phaeacians; Ulysses, shipwrecked, has not yet been recognized:

He ended and passed to his throne beside King Alcinous. The servers were mixing wine and distributing meats. The herald drew near, leading Demodocus the sweet singer whom te people honoured into the midst of the feasters; he set him there with his back to a tall column: and to the herald wily Odysseus called, having cut off from the chine of a white-toothed boar (there was abundance and to spare) a piece rich all round with fat. "Herald," said he, "take and offer this portion of flesh to Demodocus that he may eat it with a greeting from me that not even the depth of my misfortunes can chill; for it is right that bards should receive honour and reverence from every man alive, inasmuch as the Muse cherishes the whole guild of singers and teaches to each one his rules of song."

When the hero had made an end of speaking, the herald bore his meat in hand to Demodocus who received it and rejoiced. All stretched out and helped themselves to the ready cheer; and when they were filled with drink and food then Odysseus addressed Demodocus. "Demodocus, I laud you above all mortal men: I know not if it was the Muse, daughter of Zeus, that taught you, or Apollo himself. Anyhow you have sung the real history of the mishaps of the Achaeans, their deeds, their sufferings, their griefs, as if you had been there or had heard it from eye witnesses. But now change your theme and sing of how Epeius with the help of Athene carpentered together that great timber horse, the crafty device, which wise Odysseus got taken into the citadel after packing it with the men who were to lay Troy waste. Tell me all this in order, and then I will maintain everywhere that the God's grace has conferred the bounty of inspiration on your singing."

So he said; and the minstrel, fired by the God, gave proof of his mastery.

The Odyssey, vii

Cithara players (fifth century B.C.)

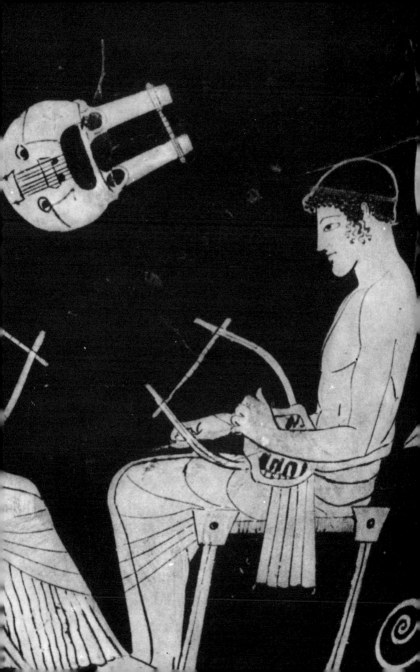

A bard signs his work

I borrow from the Homeric Hymn to Apollo, *the end of its first part, dedicated to Delos. The poet addresses the young girls of the island. This text, difficult to date, could be set between* The Iliad *and* The Odyssey, *at the beginning of the seventh century:*

> All Hail, and remember me in future days
> when one of those earthly men, looking like
> a stranger marked by life's ordeals, will ask:
> "Young ladies, which of your poets, here, is
> master of sweetness, giving greatest joy?"
> Then, speaking of us in one loud voice, cry:
> "The blind man of Chios, rugged island –
> his songs will reign in all the years to come:
>   yes, all of his songs!"

Homeric Hymn to Apollo

NOTES

1. *Sing, goddess, the anger . . .*, first words of *The Iliad*.
2. Samuel Eliot Bassett, *The Poetry of Homer*, Sather Classical Lectures, 15 (University of California Press, 1938).
3. *Clio*, Pléiade edition, *Oeuvres en prose* (1909-1914), p. 252.
4. For Dörpfeld's Troy VI: 190 meters (including the thickness of the walls) by 140 meters, 500 meters circumference, 15,000 square meters of habitable surface(this last figure from Charles Vellay, *Revue des Etudes Homériques*, vol. II, 1932, p. 51).
5. In France, Charles Vellay, *Nouveaux aspects de la question de Troie* (1930); *Controverses autour de Troie* (1936). More recently, in the United States, Rhys Carpenter, *Folk Tale, Fiction and Saga in the Homeric Epics*, Sather Classical Lectures, 20, chapter III.
6. Rhys Carpenter, *op cit*. pp. 35-38.
7. Pausanias (II, XVI) saw them at the end of the second century A.D. The Cyclops in question are not those of *The Odyssey*.
8. *Homer and the Monuments* (London, 1950), p. 452.
9. Cf. Charles Picard, *Sur le travail poétique d'Homère* (Mélanges Henri Grégoire, 1941), pp. 488-502.
10. Lorimer, *op. cit*. p. 453. And previously, in the same direction, P. Nilsson, *Homer and Mycenae* (London, 1933), p. 138.
11. In 1939 Blegen and Kourouniotis found at Pylos some six hundred tablets; later the same Blegen and Marinatos found another three hundred in continuing the digging on the site in 1952. These clay tablets were baked by the palace fire. Their authors used the latest type of Cretan script, known as linear B. The deciphering, after various attempts, was made possible after 1953 by Michael Ventris (died in an accident September 6, 1956) and John Chadwick. The most recent account of their common labors is given by their *Documents in Mycenaean Greek* (Cambridge University Press, 1956).
12. Book VII. The wine brought from Lemnos is not distributed to the army by a high command which, in fact, does not exist. The soldiers buy it individually. The supreme commander receives the "honorific share" which permits him to accumulate a real stockpile (IX).

13 Denys Page, *The Homeric Odyssey* (Oxford, 1955), p. 146; and, by the same author, *Sappho and Alcaeus* (1955), p. 177 *et seq*. One must also take into account the Greek monarchies on Cyprus, though they were more remote from the Ionian world.

14 *Sappho*, fg. 27. *Edition des Universités de France* (Th. Reinach) p. 212.

15 Xerxes led into Europe several squadrons of Libyan chariots, during the invasion of 480. (Herodotus, VII, 86).

16 Luigia Achillea Stella, *Il poema d'Ulisse* (Florence, 1955), while according more emphasis than I do to the close connections between the epic and the Mycenaean world, underlines at the same time these Oriental relationships, pp. 12-25.

17 An observation of Aristotle's, in the *Poetics*, 1449 a.

18 Which is why Meillet could write such a work as *The Indo-European Origins of Greek Meters:* the work appeared in 1923, but retains all its original value today.

19 This is one reason, among others, which keeps us from adopting all the theses of an otherwise suggestive book, Charles Autran's *Homère et les Origines sacerdotales de l'épopée grecque,* 3 vols., appearing from 1938 to 1943.

20 The ancients felt this so strongly that they refrained, when oratorical prose was enriched with certain rhythmic elements, from including among them sections of hexameter whose effect would have been almost as disparate as that of two or three sung measures in a modern speech.

21 L. Renou, *Sanskrit et Culture* (Paris, 1950), p. 37.

22 One must therefore be on guard against the temptation to imagine the bard resembling a (modern) actor who would vary his voice, his gestures, and his face according to the characters and passions he interprets. It is just as likely that the ideal of the reciter was, on the contrary, a hieratic majesty.

23 Almost 3,000 run-ons, according to Bassett, *op. cit.* p. 154.

24 I am thinking of the attempts of Charles Autran to find Tamoul (a Dravidian language of India) on the shores of the ancient Aegean,

or of the way Berard derived pre-Hellenic names from a Phoenician fabricated from the Hebrew of the Bible.

25 Thus the work of R. B. Onians, *The Origins of European Thought About the Body, the Mind, the World, Time, and Fate* (Cambridge, 2nd edition, 1954).

26 Milman Parry, *l'Épithète traditionelle dans Homère* (Paris, 1928), p. 21; by the same author, *Les Formules et la Métrique d'Homère* (Paris, 1928). This American scholar wrote these two works in French, as theses for a French doctorate.

27 M. Parry. *Les formules* ... p. 6.

28 Elizabeth M. Fraser, *La Mort de Solon* (Paris, 1949); cf. particularly the examples grouped on pp. 29-31.

29 For instance the *discours superflues* in a sentence which constitutes an alexandrine: "Tous ces discours sont superflues: il faut qu'il meure" (III, IV).

30 François Rostand, *L'imitateur de soi chez Corneille* (Paris, 1946): approximately 250 repetitions of whole lines, 500 of shorter locutions. What would a similar study of Lope de Vega show – a monster to whom some 510 plays have been credited, and who claimed to have written 2,000?

31 Eschinus, *Contra Timarcus*, 129.

32 When Mr. Parry goes so far as to say that Homer "never had to search for the words for some idea which had not previously been expressed, so that the question of originality in style meant nothing for him," he is committing an amusing error which Bassett has drawn attention to (*op. cit.* p. 18). At this rate "if the long succession of bards which preceded him had never been more original than he, *none* of Homer's ideas would ever have been expressed!" Someone had to start. Why should Homer alone not be entitled to creative genius?

33 This name is related to a verb which means *to sew*.

34 *Les Origines des Chansons de Geste. Théories et discussions* (Paris, 1951), p. 228.

35 H. T. Wade-Gery, *The Poet of The Iliad* (Cambridge, 1952), pp. 12, 13.

36 *Dialogue de l'histoire et de l'âme charnelle*, Pléiade edition, p. 310.

37 Book V.

38 P. Guillon, *Littérature de la Grèce Antique, dans l'Histoire des Littératures*, vol. I, p. 353, Encyclopédie de la Pléiade (Paris, 1955).

45

View of Argos from the Lion Gate →

OUR BROTHERS OF THE ILIAD

Zeno to the contrary, we prove movement by walking. And against the dismantlers of *The Iliad*, we prove its unity by reading it, better still: by living it. It is the least "disincarnated" work in the world: everything is in movement, blood boiling or flowing, breasts swelling or breathing their last; the gods themselves strike – and are struck; fire and water momentarily confront each other, in hand to hand combat. The murmur of crowds, the cries of battle, the noise of argument leave only a few rare moments of silence, moments of a strange solemnity. One is either altogether carried away by this world "full of sound and fury," and begins to run and shout oneself; or else, reading a motionless text with the eyes alone, one is obliged to understand nothing.

"Do you know anything more boring than *The Iliad*?," Paul Valéry once asked André Gide. And had not the same interlocutor declared to the same listener, thirty years before: "It is impossible nowadays to understand the feelings of a Homeric hero."?[1] Exactly: Paul-Ambroise, one suspects, has difficulty communicating with Achilles, and even with Ulysses. His detachable-collar mind does not accept Pallas, as she appears at the hour of battle. Moreover, should he encounter the goddess, Valéry would not recognize her: he has no third eye.

49

Achilles and his horse (Acropolis Museum, Athens)

"The murmurs of crowds, the cries of battle,
the violence of argument . . ."

Our times have again confronted us with the most elementary
necessities: with hunger, thirst, and raw desire; with our own
interior darkness, too, and the waves that flow across it.
Violent death lies everywhere in ambush; captivity, even
slavery have become everyday realities again. Many men
besides Achilles have believed their lives would be cut off
early and without warning. We have seen enough of the world
to know that there are still countries where security depends
on readiness to strike and skill in dissimulating. Raving luna-
tics, whom the divine *ate* inspires to excess and retribution,
have been heard at the heads of entire nations. Perhaps, finally,
we may have felt upon us the hand of an unknown power
warning us at the brink of error or destruction. Had we turned
about quickly enough, like Achilles, we might have seen the
goddess. At least we know that *ascesis* sharpens the senses of
the soul. A ghost from his birth, Monsieur Teste, Paul-

Ambroise's idol, has no longer even the fugitive existence of the Shades for us. It is Homer and his people who are *there*: the heroes and the indistinct *laos* [2] – all, our brothers.

Achilles, or death unopposed

Returning to *The Iliad* during the last world war, minds formed by philosophic meditation and prizing the highest values of human consciousness found themselves in agreement on this notion: "the real hero, the true subject, the center of *The Iliad*, is force." [3] It is true that we do not *feel The Iliad* unless we have submitted to its frenzied force, but it is not fair to forget that in the author's mind (who after all knew what he wanted to say) his theme is the anger of Achilles and, as the outcome proves, the anger of Achilles both satisfied and *surmounted*. Confronted with Priam, the hero abandons his

51

pursuit of vengeance upon Hector's body (and therefore upon his soul: he learns from Patroclus himself, appearing after death, that without funerary honors, a shade must wander forever before the gates of Hades). He is not unaware that the gods desire this appeasement, but he agrees *freely* to obey them: if Priam importuned him, he could "disobey the decrees of Zeus." [4] The author of *The Iliad* has chosen to glorify Achilles' *arétè*, a word for which there is no adequate translation, indicating a mixture of native superiority and excellence developed by life, in the realm of the heart as well as that of physical force.

Among all the heroes gathered beneath the walls of Troy, he has elected the one who has isolated himself from the rest in giving his free consent to an imminent and certain death (his mother, who tells him of it, is a goddess, and cannot be mistaken). Not that Homer makes his hero express this acceptance directly. Achilles even threatens to return to his ships, which would save him; but this is only a stray impulse in the face of human injustice. Does he himself believe he will leave? All his behavior indicates that his choice is made. He will resist only a death unworthy of him, the death he fears, for a moment, to find in the waters of the overflowing Xanthus: "like a swineherd swept away by the torrent when he crossed it during a storm." [5]

In mentioning Achilles' free consent, I do not suppose for a moment that Homer has set himself the "problem of free will," as the philosophical treatises call it. Among the Greek thinkers themselves, this notion takes shape only much later. Yet there is no doubt that Homer differentiates clearly between those who tremble before the destiny they have awaited blindly and those who keep their eyes open, their hearts firm. The reader has no difficulty seeing which the poet respects.

Achilles, then, is a man apart: the other combatants run the risk of death; he expects it, tomorrow, with complete certainty. But since he gives himself to death only in exchange for an *immortal* and pure glory, he can endure nothing which diminishes this glory: neither that Agamemnon, against every justification, should wrest from him the captive he has received, nor that Patroclus' loss should remain unavenged. The approach of death is not, for him, a moment of superior serenity when human passions fade away; it is the realization of his true nature, entirely consecrated to the destruction of whatever limits it. The genius of the poet is to have stopped the action at the unhoped-for moment when, under the inspiration of the gods, Achilles restrains his devouring fury. Tomorrow, once the truce of Hector's funeral games is over, Achilles will return to the slaughter. Were the poem to continue, it would bog down in the sad reaches of blood and corpses.

If we consider the extraordinary condition of this man, we understand why nothing deters him after the first affront. The outcome of the war does not matter to him. The Trojans have done nothing to him and could not threaten his country. Menelaus' cause means nothing to his family. He is here only to please Agamemnon.[6] But on the other hand, this man – swiftest, strongest, bravest, wisest in battle – cannot be restrained; nothing can win him home or toward peace. Once, he thinks of the son he has left at Scyros, but he does not even bother to name his mother. When someone reminds Briseis, the captive, that Achilles may one day make her his wife, it is not he but Patroclus. When Achilles, in the heat of discussion, declares his heartfelt love for her,[7] we wonder if polemical necessity has not made him give his amorous disappointment more conviction than he ordinarily employs. Hear Patroclus, who knows him better than anyone else: "You were born of the shimmering sea, and of the inaccessible cliffs, so inexorable is your spirit."[8] This is a goddess' son who never suckled on human milk.

I would have the reader take Achilles' divine parentage quite seriously. His mother lives in the depths of Ocean, near her father (an Old Man of the Sea), and carried her child in a womb not nourished by blood like our own. Then she left him. It is the banished Phoïnix who has cared for the royal prince in his early years, bestowing upon him the love he would have given his own son, had the gods permitted him to have one. When Thetis rises from the waves like a mist (perhaps not yet having assumed corporeal form), she is answering a cry of distress from Achilles. A mother of pain, of tears, she can prophesy only death to her son. It is she who comes to him to take his head in her hands. It is not Achilles who makes – who *can* make – the first gesture of affection. From immortal to mortal neither blood, breath, nor knowledge of invisible things has been transmitted, nor any common hope. Their natures cannot communicate; the river of death is deep

53

enough, despite Mallarmé, to separate them forever.[9] Achilles can obtain from divine hands, by Thetis' intervention, the most wonderful weapons, and from the king of the gods himself the punishment of the Achaeans. Yet the most abandoned child on earth never found himself such a stranger to his mother.

Alone, Achilles can sympathize with his aged father's loneliness. But of all those around him, this loveless man cares for only one person, Patroclus. What link binds these two men together? The most obvious, the most Greek explanation is the one that must be rejected first: there is no question of carnal love between them. If they sleep in the same tent, it is at opposite ends, each with the captive of his choice. Like all Homeric characters, they obey the great laws of nature without complications or complexes, in the simplicity of a flesh untroubled by the spirit. For Homer, there are no sexual problems. "Nothing is as pure as Homer." [10]

Patroclus, though slightly older, is neither a "big brother" nor, still less, a simple confidant. Achilles and he have grown up together, united by the natural involvement that associates boys of similar age against the encroachments of grown-ups. Together they took lessons from the centaur Chiron. Together, still, they proceeded to the lessons of war, and this time it is Achilles, the stronger of the two, who assumes the role of protector. Without the need for confidences, for sympathy, even, sometimes, for words,[11] they understand each other, support each other, draw breath for each other. Especially since the experience of Troy, who can come between them? Achilles has only Patroclus on whom to lean; Patroclus has no affection except for Achilles. Patroclus' shade will demand that their ashes be mingled in the same urn.

This admirable communion, the highest degree of friendship, will be easily recognized by all who have experienced it in their youth. But in Achilles, under the shadow of death, it reaches a pitch where it becomes identified with the passion for his own glory. At the moment he finally permits Patroclus to go to the aid of the Greek army, he ends his remarks with this strange and terrible prayer:

> Father Zeus, Athene and Apollo, if only
> not one of all the Trojans could escape destruction, not one
> of the Argives, but you and I could emerge from the slaughter
> so that we two alone could break Troy's hallowed coronal.
>
> *The Iliad*, xvi

54

We alone victors, and let the universe perish! The extremity of love, but addressed to whom? Once Patroclus falls, Achilles admits he accords him "more worth than any other of his comrades, as much as he sets upon his own head." [12] Here is the truth, hitherto unspoken, and probably never admitted to himself. In Patroclus, Achilles loved himself. He found himself in his friend, only more human, more lovable. Achilles dead, Patroclus would serve as a father to his son, a facsimile of Achilles. And this is why, having just lost his double, he considers, without any emotional paradox, that the blow is harder for him to bear than the death of his father or of this son himself. Nothing will be too much to give his friend's soul its eternal rest, not even the lives of twelve Trojan prisoners, an unprecedented sacrifice which horrifies the poet himself.

Have I gone too far, then, in claiming that the bard has wanted to glorify Achilles' *arétè*? No, for there is Book XXIV, the meeting with Priam and the final obedience to the voice of the gods. No again, because Homer has the rectitude – the innocence, so to speak – which does not recoil before the whole truth, and believes that one is not dishonored by following to its end a nature that cleaves to greatness. The extremity of excellence, where it finishes in its own destruction, is as deserving of expression as the most dazzling moments of its ascent.

On war

Hence *The Iliad* is Achilles, absent or present, since everything depends first on what he does not do, then on what he does. But there is also the war – to such a degree, and in so powerful a synthesis, that in all antiquity there is no other epic which is truly about war. The Cyclic Poems which develop the Theme of Troy alongside it have completely disappeared, and we cannot attribute their annihilation entirely to chance: something would have survived from a debris of such extent, even if only quotations, if they had had any merit alongside *The Iliad*. They were no longer copied, no longer quoted because they were insipid by comparison. [13]

Here is war *par excellence*, war as the Greeks were obliged to conceive it down through the ages: war against the Asiatics (I do not call them Barbarians, for the word is not Homeric). The *true* war, for it was the only kind that seemed to them entirely legitimate and did not disturb their conscience.[14] But *The Iliad* is the true war in another sense as well: the truth of all wars.

I must ask the modern reader who wishes to feel the sweep of *The Iliad* to forget the feelings he has cultivated about war, whatever they are. For the bard, war is not material for theories or sentimentality. It is not a Judgment of God (though the gods wage it) or of History: it does not take the *direction* of an evolution, good or bad. It does not assume the divine rhythm of destruction and creation. In this respect *The Iliad* is remote from the *Bhagavad Gita*; but it is no nearer to the sympathy which fills Arjuna at the moment he must kill. Death on the field of battle is a simple reality which requires no commentary. It is confronted in the same way as the other crude realities of existence: they are accepted by the very fact that life is accepted. Homeric man never renounces life; that is why he has no "problem" about death.

This does not mean he does not tremble before it when it seems difficult to escape: the bravest take to flight if they feel there is too much against them, and no one regards them as dishonored, not even they themselves. The wounded man does

not hesitate to groan. Flight, pain, death are taken *according to nature*, by a people who would not dream of trying to do better, who do not count too much on a divine power to modify in their favor the ordinary facts of this nature (we cannot speak yet of natural laws). Actually, certain heroes are sometimes rescued by divine hands. But even the most protected among them does not feel entirely reassured, even after a prayer followed by a favorable omen.

Considered thus, as a great phenomenon of nature, difficult for everyone at one time or another, painful for many, war is governed, at the level of man-to-man confrontation, by the law of the stronger. Such at least are the appearances as long as we do not see the supernatural background of events. It is here that *The Iliad* puts force at the center of reality.

I may be accused of bloodthirstiness if I point out to the comfortable citizens of our narrow Occident – an island still curiously privileged despite its sufferings, where men live by curious illusions, many of which, despite all experience to the contrary, are not yet overcome – it is salutary to recall the existence of force at the center of things. Our well-policed society has survived in the shelter as well as in the shadow of

Games in honor of Patroclus (National Museum of Athens)

The Trojan Horse, Massias expansion (Bibliothèque Nationale, Paris)

force. I am of Pascal's opinion: "Force is the ruler of the world, and not opinion." "Force is easily recognizable and without dispute." No nature without force. No divine action without some kind of force. The problem (Pascal once again) is to "unite force and justice." [15] But justice, law, liberty – though you embellish them with gleaming capitals – are, without force, phantom notions good only to dazzle empty minds. Homer, on this point, is salutary because he is true.

The Trojans need not be ashamed to use force, for they are defending their homes. But the Greeks need be no more ashamed, as some of them are fighting in Menelaus' cause, fulfilling their duty as allies or as "satellites"; and others, like Achilles, performing a gesture of courtesy and solidarity for Agamemnon's sake. And this, again, is the truth of all wars: no belligerent believes himself without a legitimate reason for fighting.

Homer, in consequence, as has often been pointed out, keeps the balance virtually equal between the two sides. This is praiseworthy; an Asian Greek could not have harbored too many sympathetic feelings for the true Asiatics: neighbors feared for their numbers, somewhat despised for their manners and their lesser military value. Yet the Trojan camp receives from the poet's hands its fair share of exploits and sympathetic heroes. It is treated with the epic's magnificent courtesy. How many of our contemporaries could benefit from the example!

The combat itself is not always a constant parade of ferocity. If we follow closely the several days of battle narrated, we are struck by the ceremonial character of the encounters between the great leaders. Each arrives in his chariot, hands the reins to his driver, steps down and advances toward his adversary. Possibly, they already know each other by sight; in this case, calling out by name, they invite each other to direct combat. If they do not know each other, they introduce themselves, and may mutually recognize the existence of a sacred relationship, such as hereditary hospitality, which prevents them from bearing arms against each other. The dialogue between Diomedes and Glaucos, translated at the end of this chapter, is quite representative of such high courtesy, superior to the necessities of war. Today both men would be sent before a firing squad! Diomedes and Glaucos exchange their arms without fighting, but Hector and Ajax, after fighting until nightfall, give each other gifts, so that it can be said:

Menelaus and the Trojan warriors (Berlin)

Both, in truth, fought to end the heart-devouring dispute;
But before separating, they had cemented a fair agreement.

Ajax and Achilles gambling (Vatican Museum)

Such is war waged among noble spirits, when no private rancor enters into it. Even in the fray, the loser who asks for mercy is often spared and ransomed (the captured women are kept in the Greek camp, but not the prisoners of war, apparently, even for forced labor). So that the total impression of cold ferocity *The Iliad* may leave on a reader who has been through it only once derives chiefly from the last books, where Achilles' rage for vengeance compels everyone to destruction.

Of course the technique of narrative tends to isolate and focus on the actions of the great heroes. This was the best way of interesting the hearer in a series of episodes whose continuous recitation ran the risk of some monotony; the best way, too, of glorifying all who deserved it. Thus we have, in turn, Diomedes' day; Ulysses' and Diomedes' night raid; Hector's retaliation; the resistance of the two Ajaxes, Patroclus' sortie; and finally, the long day of Achilles. And many times, alongside the greatest, other leaders share the spotlight for a moment. But this narrative procedure does not much distort the reality of combat. The common soldiers are not likely to confront the celebrated warriors directly; sometimes we even have the impression that they lay down their arms to admire the two champions. The fall of a leader inevitably involves a rout. The fray turns into a stampede, until some man with a powerful voice appears, to call the fugitives back to order. The heroes are not just the strongest men; they are the only ones capable of accounting for their behavior in action.[16] Not that they all excel in making favorable plans. Achilles, fed by rage, wants to lead the army into battle before it has eaten; it is Ulysses, the good captain, who reminds him of the stomach's needs. Nestor, a specialist in chariots, on one occasion gives some advice as to their *practical use*; his advice is valid for his own men, but is not followed. It is at the moment when the battalions leave camp that they present the splendid order the poet delights in describing; soon nothing is left of it. Homer, like Stendhal and Tolstoy, does not see operations developing "as planned."

It is at moments of darkest confusion, particularly during the routs, that the massacres occur. Achilles no longer heeds supplications. He acts by the law of death, which he accepts for himself.[17] He refuses the dying Hector the last consolation of funeral rites; but Hector had condemned Patroclus to the dogs and vultures. Achilles may not know it, but the listeners do, and are not offended by this reprisal. At these moments, the combatants are men *possessed by passion*.[18] Here again, Homer is faithful to the truth of human nature.

The Iliad, if I remember correctly, furnishes only one murder committed in cold blood; this occurs during the night reconnaissance of Book X (an action characterized as extraordinary, and on which the two heroes venture only under the protection of a goddess). The two Achaeans cannot hamper themselves with the Trojan, Dolon, whom they have captured; but Ulysses, to make him talk, has *almost* promised him his life. It is true – a Hellenic subtlety – that it is Diomede, who had said nothing during the entire interrogation, who kills him!

This is how Homer views war. Without complacence, without disgust, without lowering his eyes. We have the sense that he has really experienced it, and often enough to become hardened to it. If he described it by hearsay and purely epic tradition, would he achieve such an absence of "literature"? Would he have this variety of episodes, this multiplicity of details which, in the battle scenes, often save him from monotony?

The camp against the city

The Greek camp, by its nature, constitutes a society of men; and the presence of the captive women does not affect the fact

that each man, in his moments of weariness or fear, can find moral support only in a friend or brother. Agamemnon, with the insensitivity of a man marked by destiny, may well proclaim he prefers Chryseis to his wife, but there is no evidence that he or anyone else seeks counsel or comfort from a captive. Achilles alone has the privilege of being able to see his mother again, but as we know, it is only in order to hear her remind him of his fatal destiny. Fundamentally, each man lives alone in this cramped collectivity which would be quite untenable without a most praiseworthy natural courtesy. Those who are familiar with the thousand and one ceremonies of old Oriental societies, where the mixture of refinement and sudden barbarism was similar, have no doubts, here again, as to the truth of Homer.

This profound isolation is expressed by the poet in one of his most penetrating lines, apropos of the weeping captive women: "Supposedly for Patroclus, but each for her own woes."

Their masters are not much better off.

Troy itself is neither closely besieged nor even, at the start, blockaded from a distance. Confronting the Greeks, it furnishes the image of a complete society, with *real* women, children, old men. Although the action is shifted there quite seldom, these contrasts are enough to oppose one world to another.

Is this to satisfy the epic tradition, which at first was limited to the struggles of the Hellenic tribes among themselves? Is it from that instinct to refer everything to themselves so often manifested by peoples still unconscious of the world around them? Or is it that Homer does not conceive of the Trojans as fundamentally different from the Greeks; they have the same gods, the same language (the two sides communicate without interpreters), the same clothes, similar customs – aside from Priam's harem. It is their own home life the Greeks can divine behind the enemy ramparts; and the hearer who passes through the gates with the poet cannot miss the sweetness of the hearth. Books III and IV offer us such genre scenes. In Books XXII and XXIV, the affliction that invades the city after the loss of its defender already casts across it the shadow of the final disaster. So that from Troy, throughout the poem, falls a light softer and more mournful than the flames and shadows rising from the Greek camp.

Because of the famous scene at the Scaian Gate, where he meets Andromache and their son (Book VI), and because of

Helen's gratitude to him, Hector incarnates courage embellished by humanity. Perhaps, too, we sympathize with him for experiencing fear in battle, whereas Achilles does not feel a moment's trepidation, save when confronting the overwhelming Scamander. Hector, too, is the man who protects the women and children of Troy and seeks only their safety in the war:

Hector's farewell to Andromache (Würzburg)

he is ready to make peace at the expense of Paris, whose cowardice and sensuality he criticizes severely, to the public delight. Lastly, he is one of those whom death puts in a favorable light: it creates the unanimity of his people in grief; it provokes the intervention of the gods to save his body; it even forces from the poet a belated admission that he was hand-

some. Thus at the end everything is forgotten: the brusqueness with which Hector treats everyone, the fashion contrary to the "law" [19] with which he wears Achilles' armor – which Apollo had caused to fall from the body of Patroclus – and his desire to mutilate his fallen victim.

Troy also gains an edge through Priam, particularly from the grandeur with which he humiliates himself before Achilles in order to obtain his son's body. Compared with Nestor, an old man still on the field of battle and who kills his man there, Priam is an ancient overwhelmed by years and by fate. He appears reluctantly between the armies to conclude a truce; his only words (six lines) are to declare that he cannot bear to witness a battle between Paris and Menelaus, though nothing of what follows indicates he loves Paris. All the more merit is due him for facing Achilles, though during the entire adventure we see him trembling with terror. This was once a fierce warrior, but the decay of his body has affected his courage. His age, at least, allows him to feel a certain indulgence: he does not blame Helen; he knows we are pushed by forces more powerful than ourselves. Probably – another effect of senility – he feels no more than one deep emotion, that which attaches him to Hector, the strongest and most handsome of his sons, the true rampart of the realm, and his own shield against a humiliating death to which he cannot resign himself.

The shadows rise around Troy. The entire city is widowed by Hector. The society of spears, of men alone in camp, is to conquer this world of families and fortifications. Achilles expects nothing but premature death which, on the scales of destiny, is to raise the balance of his glory. This is the progress of *The Iliad*.

The gods and destiny

This is the progress of *The Iliad* on earth. But the scene in the heavens offers no less tumultuous contrast: it is as im-important to the action as the death and passions of men. There is no epic without theology.

The reader must abandon the vague mythological recollections of his schooldays – they are winnowed chaff. Our formal instruction offers as little understanding of religions as of poetry: everything deepest and most disturbing about our inner life escapes its grasp. It is into this region of obscure

71

Achilles' funeral, fragment (Louvre)

palpitations, of sudden questionings, that we must advance, and
nothing takes us further off the track than trying to introduce
into Homer's religious notions an intellectual coherence which
has no hope of reflecting the realities. What the poet knows
from experience is that life is full of unexpected inspirations,
sometimes salutary, sometimes pernicious, which we are unable
to feel responsible for. We must therefore attribute them,
according to their importance, either to an undifferentiated
divine power, some *daimon*, or to a more personalized god.
It is not only a question of major decisions which engage
existence as a whole, but of a contest won, a lucky move which
permits us to avoid a blow: everything extraordinary is supernatural.[20]

The extraordinary within us first of all, which offers most
constraints. The extraordinary world of dreams in particular.
The latter, we know, play an important part in the Homeric
epic. Whether the bard has recourse to the image of the
nightmare in which one cannot seize what one pursues, though
the pursued never disappears altogether, or whether he empha-
sizes the pathetic aspect of dreams in which we meet the dead
dear to us, he draws on the most direct dream experience. On
the other hand, when the personified Dream inspires Agamemnon with a deceptive confidence only for the needs of
action, we feel as unconvinced as wise Nestor.[21] Yet even this
account includes one line which renders in the most lifelike
way the slow emergence of the mind from the dream: "He
wakened, but the sound of the divine voice surrounded him
still."

72

In the world outside the self, the divine can appear at any moment, and in the most unexpected guises. A bird flies off at a critical moment: sometimes it is a god, sometimes merely a sign he sends. A meteor is a great sign; yet Pallas, falling from the sky between the enemy lines, also assumes this guise. Henceforth, who can tell in such a case whether a man trembles before a wonder of nature or before divinity itself? A man distinguished by uncommon beauty or outstanding in battle for his courage is, or might be, a god, before whom one must stand astonished, and, above all, whom one must not strike. Pandarus thinks he recognizes Diomedes in the fray, but prudently adds: "It is not certain, after all, I don't know that it's not a god." [22]

What signals the approach of the supernatural is generally that rapture which combines fear, admiration, and total adoration, which takes away breath as well as speech, and which the Greeks call *thambos*. Father Festugière has spoken eloquently about this, and there is no need to embroider the matter.[23] When a hero is befriended by a divinity, he can see it, and recognize it, though it is invisible to all others. By what? Sometimes by its outward appearance. A controversial line refers to the brilliance of the divine eyes; at least, this is the way it has often been read. But is a visible sign indispensable? In any case, most men would find it difficult to endure the direct sight of a divinity; it is Hera herself who shrieks: "Terrible are the gods in their fiery manifestations!" [24]

I cannot imagine what Pierre Mazon's notions of an inner life are, but when he writes of Homeric society that it "can scarcely have had any very deep religious feelings," and that in fact "there was never a poem less religious than *The Iliad*," [25] I am frankly revolted by such curt certitudes. If only our contemporaries possessed the sense of hidden *being*, of the invisible presence, which in their own way the beliefs of the Homeric age attest, and if only they too could tremble before the fire of the theophanies (I mean: before certain illuminations in the depths of our inner darkness). Is it not the same movement which bears the soul toward the same essence, through the impersonal *daimons*, the anthropomorphic gods, the god "sensible of heart," and He who is beyond being and non-being?

I am not at all sure that Homeric anthropomorphism, since that is what is in question here, is "a form of rationalism." [26] The god in man's image is also man in the form of a god, a dream consubstantial with our nature, a nature well aware, when it consults only its spontaneous impulse, that it has been created for something other than its present prison. "Rising from memory" to the primary contemplation of "the essence which by essence is essence," to quote Plato, metaphysician of our primordial dreams.[27] "Hence the body of glory desires beneath the body of mud." [28]

What, then, for Homer is the god in man's image? In one sense, a transcending being. Apollo affirms the fact:

> Never of the same race
> Will be the immortal gods and the men who walk the earth.[29]

A difference illustrated by the fact that the gods do not have blood in their bodies. Any participation of one nature in the other is excluded. In the first place, there is the barrier of death. But immortality is only the extreme degree of a more general quality that sets the gods apart: their *arétè*,[30] which is not a virtue in the moral sense of the term, but that excellence in all things by which superior beings are recognized. In everything, they exceed us: in strength, of course, in swiftness (they move from the heavens to the earth in the space of a thought, scarcely more), in intelligence, and in foreknowledge (for they see the future).

But they excel in destroying as well as in preserving. Several centuries of adulterated Christianity and sentimental optimism, and perhaps also some heritage of Manicheanism have ac-

Zeus, ancient bronze

customed us to separating God and destruction. The Old Testament was more virile. Port-Royal too. India again shows us how to consider together both sides of any manifestation of being: the emergence of the creature and its return to non-being. In Homer, too, we see things whole. This is honesty. This is courage.

More powerful than we, the gods destroy better, and with absolute certainty. In the Trojan War, most of them have chosen sides. The reasons for their choices are not always clear to a modern reader, but it was not necessary to explain them to Homeric audiences: ancient connections with this or that race (Apollo, an Asiatic god, with the Trojans; Hera, with the Achaeans), special protection accorded an entire lineage, old offenses punished. They reason like feudal lords: they owe protection to their liege men. Apollo would fail to fulfill the requirements of the age's elemental morality if he did not cause the Greeks, their mules, and their dogs to die by the hundreds the moment Agamemnon treats his priest unjustly. Where would one be if one did not make oneself respected? Let us say that their transcendence ends where their passions take over, and add that human morality has formed other needs, but let us leave the "immorality" of these gods at that.

We must concede them the qualities of their defects. They save as often as they destroy – though only chosen individuals – while they destroy the multitudes with their leaders. They are faithful to their protégés, at the same time they insist on not owning their preferences too openly.[31] Further: between these chosen individuals and themselves they admit a certain affection. In a treatise on morality in the Aristotelian canon, though not by Aristotle himself, the *Magna Moralia*, we find this revealing sentence: "It would be absurd to say that one loves Zeus." [32] I suspect this is not only the notion of a philosopher, but the feeling of many enlightened Greeks in the time of Alexander. In *The Iliad*, Diomedes and Ulysses, at a critical moment, turn to their protectress, Athena, and say: "This is the moment to show that you love us." "The two of us," says the same goddess to Achilles, in a tone of complicity, at the moment they fell Hector together. Although a certain modesty keeps the worshipper from manifesting a corresponding attachment to his divinity, it goes without saying that it exists, for without it man would not be justified in expecting divine aid. Finally, the gods, even Zeus himself, are capable of

77

admitting (rarely) a feeling of compassion, even for the masses.

Friendship and compassion are naturally accorded to pious individuals. Despite the impression of uncertainty inspired by the individual wills of the gods, one has the sense that piety is useful. Hector, Priam believes, can thank his devotion to the gods for the fact that his body is neither torn nor corrupted (though the king is not surprised that it has not protected him from death); but it is this same piety which assures a victory in sporting contests. The fact is that man, to a certain degree, is capable of deserving: a cruel whim or an implacable destiny do not decide everything. But we can deal with human freedom only by speaking first of that of the gods.

There are, in fact, two degrees of difficulty: the freedom of the other gods with regard to Zeus their master; the freedom of Zeus himself (and, conjointly, of the gods and men) with regard to fate. Homer has represented Zeus rather strangely. He rules over the gods with the most muscular kind of force. On the other hand, he *knows more*; in particular, he understands the unexpressed thoughts of the other gods, a clairvoyance extremely embarrassing for them, even though it occasionally seems to be in abeyance. Nevertheless, when he threatens them, he often does not distinguish the innocent from the guilty. Hera, who knows him best of all, unhesitatingly speaks of the *acts of disaster* he is meditating.[33]

Hence he does not live in communion nor even always in society with the gods; the poet likes to show him withdrawn, retired to some mountain top, the solitary observer of men at war. Homer attributes to Zeus a thought of suggestive ambiguity:

. . . I am concerned for those who rush to their destruction.
And yet I shall remain here in a hollow of Mount Olympus,
Seated above them, and my heart delights in watching them. . . .

Is this the transposition to a god of a view of the human soul, fixed at a moment of sadism and enhanced by melancholy? Is this a trace, preserved from some infinitely remote tradition, of the cosmic joy of a god who tramples on his creature the better to re-create it? I am afraid the poem leaves us no cause for doubt: when Zeus sees the gods themselves join battle, *his heart, delighted, begins to laugh.*

This god who behaves, at times, like a genius of evil (this is

78

not Jehovah who puts his people through hardships to forge their grandeur), is nevertheless the divinity the greatest leaders invoke at critical moments, the one whom the pious Achilles declares *high and excellent among the gods.* For this was certainly the Greek practice in the Homeric period, and these were the ritual epithets. And since it would be foolhardy to declare Homer a heretic, in conscious rebellion against the cult of Zeus, it would be wiser to wonder if this is not a re-action against the Father of Heaven, imported by the Achaean invaders, on the part of the religious memory of the Aegeans, formerly consecrated to the Great Mother.[34] The union of Zeus and Hera on Gargarus – even if the poet accounts for it by an impulse of desire in the veins of the god – preserves in its setting the majesty of the ancient hierogamies of Earth and Heaven. But this reconciliation of the two traditions is immediately broken.

The gods, in dealing with their despot, possess therefore only the liberties they can wrest or purloin from him; they waver between fear and rebellion. But Zeus in his turn? He confronts a force which is not personified, which has neither history nor locale, which we call Fate and which Homer designates by the words *moïra, aïsa,* "the portion assigned to each." For man, fate spins a destiny which awaits him at birth. But how does it function with regard to the king of the gods?

It is hopeless to look for a precise answer. We know the insoluble problems imposed on a more philosophic mode of thought when it must balance divine freedom and the laws of nature, human liberty and predestination. Has not each of us felt at times the incontrovertible evidence of our freedom, and at others, with the same intensity, the pressure of overbearing forces which constrain and sometimes stifle us? Homer is no further out of this dilemma than we ourselves, and his Zeus no more than he. What is certain is that, according to *The Iliad,* Achilles *could* transgress destiny and cross the walls of Troy; Zeus *could* save Sarpedon or Hector from predestined death (at least for a while). But the possibility is not realized; and in the two cases where Zeus consults the Olympian gods, seeking to save his protégés, one of them answers him: *Do so, but we, the other gods, will not all approve what you do.* And Zeus does not insist.

Why does he hesitate, he who does not object to acting in the minority? Perhaps because of the feeling that by contra-

Hermes weighing the souls of Achilles and Memnon (Louvre)

dicting Fate he would cause some damage in the universe (not to say the universal order)? A kind of fear, mixed with modesty: these things, as we say, "aren't done."

And man remains, in any case, a sorry enough fellow. He is not promised a happy survival: the sojourn among the Dead is an *abode of dread and putrefaction, which provokes the horror of the gods themselves.* Our better part is our glory. The poet's art transmits it, as an example, to the generations to come: that is our immortality. There is no immortality for the greyish shades.

The poet's era

These are the successive levels of the stage, the hidden principles of the action, some of the characters: an epic is a drama. And indeed, all of Greek tragedy is already to be found in Homer.

The dramatic virtues of *The Iliad* are what we know best. The naturalness of the characters, the skill displayed in con-

trasting them, the ingenuity of the arguments, are common-places scarcely worth repeating. I will add one figure: out of the 16,696 lines of *The Iliad*, dialogue takes up approximately 4,800; speeches and isolated remarks 2,200.[35] Greek eloquence, too, is already in Homer. In him, as in the Athenians of Pericles' times according to Thucydides, speech and action, far from being mutually destructive, complete each other.

The Mediterranean European needs no explanation for this love of words for their own sake, for the melting savor they have in the mouth. The man of the North, examining the Homeric speeches closely, will discover that everything in them finds its justification either in the light of action or in the depths of character. It woud be an error to pass them by on

the pretext that rhetoric is the enemy of poetry. For they develop out of nature, not out of rhetoric! The fact remains that today the lover of poetry, particularly if he cannot read Homer in the original language, finds his largest satisfaction elsewhere than in the speeches, even the most moving among them.

If the poet is the man who, from his vision of the sensuous universe, creates his own universe, separating it from the first, who then was ever more of a poet than Homer? This is the man with the lightning glance. Only someone who snatches the essence of an image on the wing could imagine this fragment of conversation while one chariot passes another:

But go now, Patroclus beloved of Zeus, to Nestor
and ask him who is this wounded man he brings in from the fighting.
Indeed, seeing him from behind I thought he was like Machaon,
Asklepios' son, in all ways, but I got no sight of the man's face
since the horses were tearing forward and swept on by me.

The Iliad, xi

Only a seasoned and sensitive retina could register both the movement of the sea ruffled by a sudden wind and its color shifting at the same moment:

Even as the Zephyr sends a shudder over the water,
As soon as it rises, and the sea darkens with it.

And he was not only a past master in the manipulation of formulas, but an attentive observer as well, an artisan who out of two "clichés" juxtaposed could produce a true vision of Achilles, sitting "On the gray beach, staring at the wine-dark sea."

His glance has breadth no less than acuteness. It can focus on a fringe of seaweed on the beach, the spindrift rising from the wave, the cloud of chaff which the wind spreads around the winnowers, and it can also embrace the movement of an entire army in successive waves, or in immobility like mountain-blocked clouds. Homer delights in these massive evocations, which he knows how to deal with, if necessary, without the aid of comparison. The elite of the Greek forces waits for the enemy attack:

Locking spear by spear, shield against shield at the base, so buckler
leaned on buckler, helmet on helmet, man against man,
and the horse-hair crests along the horns of their shining helmets
touched as they bent their heads, so dense were they formed on
[each other,
and the spears shaken from their daring hands made a jagged
[battle line.
Their thoughts were driving straight ahead in the fury of fighting.

The Iliad, xiii

Homer preserves the potency of his gaze even when he turns it on the ranks. But he is above all a man who has *contemplated* at length (which is why, if we are to accept his blindness, it must be a blindness that came late in life). A long time in silence and retirement – just as he depicts Zeus himself. In

85

the heat of action, he likes to withdraw abruptly from the field of vision and shift to a solitary observer, alien to the battle, with whom our gaze plunges into remote vistas.

As from his watching place a goatherd watches a cloud move
on its way over the sea before the drive of the west wind;
far away though he be he watches it, blacker than pitch is,
moving across the sea and piling the storm before it,
and as he sees it he shivers and drives his flocks to a cavern;
so about the two Aiantes moved the battalions.

The Iliad, iv

Or else the shepherd, more humbly, appears in a corner of the picture, very small, as in our classical landscapes, but his silent joy is enough to recall, behind the nights of war, the eternal living presence of the Night.

So with hearts made high these sat night-long by the outworks
of battle, and their watchfires blazed numerous about them.
As when in the sky the stars about the moon's shining
are seen in all their glory, when the air has fallen to stillness,
and all the high places of the hills are clear, and the shoulders
                                                            [out-jutting
and the deep ravines, as endless bright air spills from the heavens
and all the stars are seen, to make glad the heart of the shepherd.

The Iliad, viii

On one occasion the poet calls on the eagle's gaze, which even from high overhead discerns the hare huddled under a bush. It is often from such a bird's-eye view that the bard describes the landscape or the scene. The experience of a shepherd or a lookout? Perhaps merely his own nature has inclined him to see this way, from the skies, what he knows so well; how to see on the ground, too, mingling with the crowd. A powerful lever of poetic transfiguration, which never gives the impression of artifice.

This art of distance and compositional shift permits the bard not only to place himself beside an observer on the scene, but also to anticipate the future and to hear in advance what will be said. Hector takes leave of Andromache: his anguished spirit already imagines the tasks his captive wife will be compelled to perform if Troy falls; this is a common enough trick of the imagination, but his is stronger, and already runs through the streets, listening:

And the day will come when someone, seeing you weeping, will say,
That one was the wife of Hector. . . .

Thus the future is no longer a possibility in the mind; already
one moves within it, already it is a reality.

The siege of Troy

Everything is real, everything is before one's eyes in the
Homeric narrative. If a contemporary writer showed the same
continuity of vision, the same uninterrupted movements of
characters and crowds before our eyes, how much we would
write about the cinematic nature of his work! *The Iliad*,
starting with its twelfth line, where we see Chryses appear with
his sacred wand and the fillets of Apollo, is a film with almost
no cuts: unless we are blind and deaf, there is not one moment

87

when we do not see or hear something. The description of the shield of Achilles, forged by Hephaistos, is also made vivid by the flux that carries all before it, which is what sets it apart from all Parnassian chiselings. Where its reliefs represent human action, they are seen in movement: the bridal procession advances *in the flare of torches*, the judges stand up to pronounce sentence, the workers come and go in the fields. Better still, the sounds rise upward (no other scene combines so many different ones): the wedding song, the cries of the hearers during the sessions, the shepherds' flutes, the *phormynx* of the child leading the harvesters' dances, and even the howling of the dogs, the bellowing of the bull slaughtered by lions.

The *real* shield has been forgotten long since, but the entire life of humanity: family, laws, arms, work, and play, in one hundred and fifteen lines, is carved at white heat upon the metal.

The world, the elements, and the poet's visions

The shield of Achilles sums up "the wise meditations" of the god who has created it. The human scenes are surrounded by Ocean, the border of the shield, the Earth-Ocean, is supernatural: Hera herself describes it (Book XIV) as the origin of the gods. Somewhere, in the inner section (perhaps at the center), the divine artist has modeled the earth, the sky, the sea, the sun, the moon, and the chief constellations. Such "meditations" are clear enough: man is not separate from the universe; his life is set in this entirety (I avoid the word *cosmos*, for in Homer the word has not yet acquired its philosophical sense). The word harmony is not in the text, but this entire series of scenes evokes it so naturally that Jaeger is quite justified in writing: "The profound meaning of the harmony between man and nature, which inspires the description of the shield of Achilles, is predominant in Homer's notion of the world. The same great rhythm penetrates the All in motion." [36] We must not speak of "philosophy" here, but we can recognize a total sense of the world, organized into related images, if not into concepts.

In this world which no poet, however great, can encompass fully, toward which elements is the author's choice oriented? Even if we attribute a much greater importance to the epic formulas than I choose to admit, the question is still valid. For they do not provide all the elements of the long comparisons, or even of the quick sketches. Ever since the ancient commentators, we have regarded the comparisons, the pictures marginal to the narrative, as primarily "poetic ornaments." [37] This is probably the use the bard intended them for, but his choice among them is significant. Nothing, as a matter of fact, obliges him to recur so frequently to the same type of image, unless it be personal inclination. It is here, among the hidden sources of consciousness on which the imagination feeds,[38] that we must seek what is most secret in Homer.

Homer is a man of high places. Out of every four or five images, it has been noted, one takes place on a mountain-top.[39] But we must add the peaks touched by the gods in their descents to earth, and those from which they follow the action. There is, obviously, some sacred tradition which sets the union of Zeus and Hera on Gargarus; but it is the poet who admires the giant pines, enjoys the thickness and the springiness of the grass, gathers in the hollow of his hand the drops the clouds leave on the peak. At first one hesitates to bring up Olympus; it is, on the whole, a conventional site, the object of traditional formulas which neither describe it nor suggest its realities; or else, as in Book VIII, with its gates, its stables where the chariots are lined up, each beneath its cover and on its platform, with its thrones and couches, it scarcely differs from a human palace. But the imagination is often reminded of its aerial situation by the flights of the gods.

Yet it is hard to believe that the poet who has had the experience of running in dreams has not had that of flight as well. Nothing of this is suggested in those cases where the Olympian gods swoop down upon us as birds of prey; this is an extremely old tradition expressed by the inevitable formulas. But there is a greater dream power in the flight of the divine horses which

> ... Both, without hanging back, took flight
> Into that region between the earth and the starry sky.

And when this man, who has contemplated the clouds and derived from their movements, from their immobility, and from their shadows so many effects of chiaroscuro, represents Ares mounting the skies with them,

Even as a vapor rises above the clouds, pure shadow,
When a grieving wind rises out of the heat of day.

we must realize that he has mused under the stormclouds and
let his thoughts rise with them, as he has delighted in the heavy
snow or the autumn rains.

If he loves mountain peaks, it is because among them one
is near the airy sites which myths, shamanic visions, dreams of
sleep and waking consistently show, down through the ages and
across continents, to be so necessary to the human spirit. It is
here that man encounters the stars whose sight fills the shepherd
with ecstasy, from here we see the "thrice desired" night fall.
It is here, above all, that man encounters the gods; and their
instantaneous flight from one region to the other, from earth
to the heavens, is that of the soul which tears itself from its
limitations.

Often, from the heights, the bard's thought descends to the
sea. More often, certainly, than the subject, being a land
action, requires. Confronted by the sea, Homer does not feel
the presence of a fraternal spirit. He has not seen it smiling,
save around the god Poseidon, alone capable of ruling it, and
that is a rather artificial tableau. The cave where Hephaistos
takes shelter with the marine goddesses is pure dream-stuff
(reminding one of the maternal womb);

... And all around the Ocean's course
(Foam and murmur) flowed ineffably by....

For the ancients, as a matter of fact, all navigation implied
the anxiety of separation. Homer has said it all in four ample,
pathetic, and naked lines:

As when from across water a light shines to mariners
from a blazing fire, when the fire is burning high in the mountains
in a desolate steading, as the mariners are carried unwilling
by storm winds over the fish-swarming sea, far away from their
[loved ones.
The Iliad, xix

Similarly, rivers suggest chiefly ravage and fear to Homer.
Only the banks of the Cayster, with their flocks of water birds,
offer an image of repose, although the passage in question
illustrates an army in battle. In fact, the great phenomena of

nature are always hostile to the weakness of men. Even fog, which does no harm, is a deceptive power. Falling over part of the battlefield, it does not stop the fighting, but adds to the difficulties of the combatants – and encountering such a gratuitous incident, one wonders if the author is recalling a personal tribulation or transcribing a nightmare.

The poet is as afraid of fire as of water. He thinks immediately of a forest fire or the sack of a city. To express the frenzy and the power of Achilles, he has Hector say:

> I will go to meet him, though he have hands like fire
> – Hands like fire – and the violence of glowing iron.

As for the campfire near which the soul is comforted, it takes the fear of the sea, as we have just seen, for Homer to discover its meaning. He shows Hephaistos at work, but pays no attention to the fire of the forge.

Nowhere does he seem affected by the earth itself, its texture or its odor, nor curious about its caverns. His images remind us often enough of various rustic scenes, though it is the shepherd's life that holds first place among them. Yet his Mediterranean nature makes him a man of bread and wine: on occasion he refers to the harvests, less often to orchards, to tilling (behind the plow, the earth "blackens," the only vivid evocation of the soil), to the vineyards and grape-harvests. His heart does not beat to the rhythm of the annual round of work. When, speaking of a fallen warrior, he evokes the oak, symbol of tenacity, he always alludes to its roots, and we know how closely this image is associated with all kinds of "terrestrial archetypes." [40] Nevertheless, neither water, fire, nor earth counts, in Homer's visions, for as much as the sky of clouds and mountain-tops.

There is a share of tradition, evidently, in the custom of comparing warriors to beasts of prey, but the mere juxtaposition of the "formulary" passages with the others reveals the kind of fascination the poet has experienced with regard to the great carnivores, wolves, panthers, lions especially – the latter truly astonishing. Their number alone is indicative, but it is their variety and their vividness which gives their procession its entire significance. Not only, apparently, is Homer familiar with the habits of lions – after all, lions were common in Asia Minor – but he likes to represent them feeding, bloody and bristling, just as he enjoys describing the wounds and agonies

of warriors. Of course he brings to his descriptions of wounds an almost clinical precision, which sometimes diminishes their horror. He has a surgeon's eye, and his work, from this point of view, has been of constant interest to physicians.[41] We may assume a bent towards the profession. Yet that would not explain everything. For there is indeed an instinct which draws him to bloodshed, to the work of the ripping fang as well as of the penetrating thrust. If we must regard this as a cruel streak inhibited in life and expressed in his work, it is at least a cruelty according to nature (which has created its beasts of prey and its bloodthirsty men), a spontaneous cruelty unembellished by the imagination. In Homer there are – practice of base souls – no tortures; his heroes are noble.

He has even seen, in two of his heroes at their moments of devouring fury, a sign that is quasi-divine: a supernatural glow.[42] Diomedes receives from Athena *an inextinguishable fire* that springs out of his helmet and from his shield. A light emanates from the shield, the lance, and the whole body of Achilles in action. This is not the mere gleam of bronze, whose effect, in the other leaders, is not accentuated, as here, by comparisons of an astral order: moon and stars. Or, rather, it *is* the glitter of arms, but detached from them, living its own life, the work of the gods, generating a sacred dread. Through the natural, a kind of supernature shines. These are traditions of an extremely ancient kind, better preserved in the Irish epic, so close to Homer in its use of sacred numbers.[43] The latter attributes to the young Setanta, the future Cuchulain, when he is seized with his warlike fury, many other extraordinary phenomena, such as the appearance of a spark at the tip of each hair, a wave of fire springing from his mouth, the "heroes' moon" appearing on his forehead.[44] The line of thought is fundamentally the same, but the Ionian poet lacks a taste for the fantastic.

No sooner has one advanced this notion than one thinks of Book XXI, of Achilles' struggle against the waves of the Scamander, of Hephaistos' intervention, the combat of fire against water, a long episode where the hand of the gods is everywhere. Nothing here should be on the mortal scale. Yet we must recognize the evidence: Homer has given human guise to the helping gods, and the river hissing beneath the flames reminds him only of a basin in which hogfat is being rendered. Here we feel his limits.

Language once again

This is the moment to discuss the poem's verbal expression, to make apparent certain qualities of Homeric language which have not found their place in the preceding chapter.

There would be its quality of sound, but how speak of this

Detail from a seventh century vase (British Museum)

apart from the Greek text – and without a great deal of caution, for we may be poor judges of such things? We have to listen to the bards, and learn how an ear trained by the appreciation of long and short syllables, by the drumming of strong beats, by the musical accompaniment, would respond to them. Did such an ear possess further reserves of attention and delight for the brilliance of the vowels, the liquidity or clash of consonants? Homer, of course, did not practice systematic alliteration, essential in other methods of poetry. Sometimes, we

95

sense, he has been attracted by the explosive value of a word: thus, to present in all its thunder the entry of the gods into battle, he cries, in an image which still takes away the breath of timid commentators: "Amphi de *salpinxen* megas ouranos" ("All around, the sky burst forth with a *trumpet call* into its immensity") (XXL). But these more or less obvious cases remain rare. The ancients, who understood such things better than we, have no chapter, in their criticism, for such appreciations.

It is also impossible for us to judge with any exactitude, as only his contemporaries could, the degree of rarity of certain epithets unfamiliar even to the ancient scholiasts, some centuries later. We may say that on the whole the language of the epic, composite though it is from the point of view of dialect, is *natural*. Things and people keep their everyday names: a donkey, a dog, a pig remain donkey, dog, and pig, and there is only one word with which to say so. Actions and feelings are rendered by terms accessible to everyone. The creation of composite words in conformity with the genius of the language, far from complicating expression, makes thought more precise. The compound adjective never forms that tapestry background behind the action which we find so wearying in the Indian epic. Nor did the bards ever cultivate the riddle-periphrase, like the Scandinavian *kenningar*. So that despite its constant effort to adapt the form to the meter, sometimes moving far from the spoken language, Homeric language has many qualities of a popular tongue, in the best sense of the expression, that is, of a language not yet corrupted by scraps of literature and philosophy. Honesty and purity.

These qualities must also be understood in a deeper sense. Physical love is rendered by the notion of *mingling in tenderness* (inconceivable that it might be in indifference) and if the wounds of battle sometimes necessitate the mention of a man's sexual organs, the word designating them means that they are *worthy of respect* or *objects of respect*.[45] A healthy language, a healthy thought. No short-cuts, no circumlocutions.

If the use of formulas involves a certain stiffness, this is more than compensated for by the movement of the sentence, which arises from the breath of the thought itself. It is this internal energy which impels it from one line of verse to the next, and gives the hexameter its speech inflections. There is no greater error, consequently, than to petrify this mobility in translation in order to respect our prose syntax, or to impose on this freedom the mechanics of our traditional verse.

It would be an exaggeration to claim that the bards, despite their genius for liberty, always escape the monotonies inherent in any fixed system of versification! But it is remarkable, considering the length of the two poems, that they are so rarely dull. They succumb to monotony, as one might expect, in the sections of "fill," inevitable in a continuous narrative. It is here that the formulas are useful in getting on, but here, too, they are harmful to the creative impulse. When the poem comes back to life, the formulas are nothing more than elements of expression which assume their position in the turn of thought and which we immediately forget we have heard a moment before, even when we know them well.

From these characteristics common to the two poems, we are not forced to conclude in advance that they have a common author. Whether or not it is the same eye which has seen the adventures of Ulyssess and the exploits of Achilles, the same imagination which has set both *The Iliad* and *The Odyssey* moving, is a question that can be answered only from the depths of the text.

Courtesy: Diomedes and Glaucos

How two "knights" encounter each other, and how they recognize each other as friends:

Now Glaukos, sprung of Hippolochos, and the son of Tydeus
came together in the space between the two armies, battle-bent.
Now as these advancing came to one place and encountered,
first to speak was Diomedes of the great war cry:
'Who among mortal men are you, good friend? Since never
before have I seen you in the fighting where men win glory,
yet now you have come striding far out in front of all others
in your great heart, who have dared stand up to my spear far-
                                                    [shadowing.
Yet unhappy are those whose sons match warcraft against me.
But if you are some one of the immortals come down from the
                                                    [bright sky,
know that I will not fight against any god of the heaven. . . .
. . . but if you are one of those mortals who eat what the soil
                                                    [yields,
come nearer, so that sooner you may reach your appointed
                                                    [destruction.'
    Then in turn the shining son of Hippolochos answered:
'High-hearted son of Tydeus, why ask of my generation?
As is the generation of leaves, so is that of humanity.
The wind scatters the leaves on the ground, but the live timber
burgeons with leaves again in the season of spring returning.
So one generation of men will grow while another
dies. Yet if you wish to learn all this and be certain
of my genealogy: there are plenty of men who know it.
There is a city, Ephyre, in the corner of horse-pasturing
Argos; there lived Sisyphos, that sharpest of all men,
Sisyphos, Aiolos' son.

The Iliad, vi

This genealogy leads Glaucos to tell, in 150 lines, the legend of Bellerophon, and he concludes:

But Hippolochos begot me, and I claim that he is my father;
he sent me to Troy, and urged upon me repeated injunctions,
to be always among the bravest, and hold my head above others,
not shaming the generation of my fathers, who were
the greatest men in Ephyre and again in wide Lykia.
Such is my generation and the blood I claim to be born from.'
    He spoke, and Diomedes of the great war cry was gladdened.
He drove his spear deep into the prospering earth, and in winning

99

words of friendliness he spoke to the shepherd of the people:
'See now, you are my guest friend from far in the time of our
[fathers.
Brilliant Oineus once was host to Bellerophontes
the blameless, in his halls, and twenty days he detained him,
and these two gave to each other fine gifts in token of friendship.
Oineus gave his guest a war belt bright with the red dye,
Bellerophontes a golden and double-handled drinking-cup,
a thing I left behind in my house when I came on my journey.
Tydeus, though, I cannot remember, since I was little
when he left me, that time the people of the Achaians perished
in Thebe. Therefore I am your friend and host in the heart of
[Argos;
you are mine in Lykia, when I come to your country.
Let us avoid each other's spears, even in the close fighting.
There are plenty of Trojans and famed companions in battle
[for me
to kill, whom the god sends me, or those I run down with my
[swift feet,
many Achaians for you to slaughter, if you can do it.
But let us exchange our armour, so that these others may know
how we claim to be guests and friends from the days of our
[fathers.'
So they spoke, and both springing down from behind their
[horses
gripped each other's hands and exchanged the promise of
[friendship.
The Iliad, vi

Wild beasts

Some lions

whom the shepherd among his fleecy flocks in the wild lands
grazed as he leapt the fence of the fold, but has not killed him,
but only stirred up the lion's strength, and can no more fight him
off, but hides in the steading, and the frightened sheep are
[forsaken,
and these are piled pell-mell on each other in heaps, while the
[lion
raging still leaps out again over the fence of the deep yard.
The Iliad, v

And as a lion seizes the innocent young of the running
deer, and easily crunches and breaks them caught in the strong
[teeth

when he has invaded their lair, and rips out the soft heart from
[them,
and even if the doe be very near, still she has no strength
to help, for the ghastly shivers of fear are upon her also
and suddenly she dashes away through the glades and the timber
sweating in her speed away from the pounce of the strong beast.

The Iliad, xi

While others still in the middle plain stampeded like cattle
when a lion, coming upon them in the dim night, has terrified
the whole herd, while for a single one sheer death is emerging.
First the lion breaks her neck caught fast in the strong teeth,
then gulps down the blood and all the guts that are inward;

The Iliad, xi

As when the men who live in the wild and their dogs have
[driven
a tawny lion away from the mid-fenced ground of their oxen,
and will not let him tear out the fat of the oxen, watching
nightlong against him, and he in his hunger for meat closes in
but can get nothing of what he wants, for the raining javelins
thrown from the daring hands of the men beat ever against him,
and the flaming torches, and these he balks at for all of his fury
and with the daylight goes away, disappointed of desire.

The Iliad, xi

As two lions catch up a goat from the guard of rip-fanged
hounds, and carry it into the density of the underbrush,
holding it high from the ground in the crook of their jaws, so
two Aiantes lifted Imbrios high.   [the lordly
The Iliad, xiii

. . . Like a lion over his young, when the lion
is leading his little ones along, and men who are hunting
come upon them in the forest. He stands in the pride of his
[great strength
hooding his eyes under the cover of down-drawn eyelids.

The Iliad, xvii

Wolves attacking their quarry

And they, as wolves
who tear flesh raw, in whose hearts the battle fury is tireless,
who have brought down a great horned stag in the mountains,
[and then feed
on him, till the jowls of every wolf run blood, and then go

all in a pack to drink from a spring of dark-running water,
lapping with their lean tongues along the black edge of the surface
and belching up the clotted blood; in the heart of each one
is a spirit untremulous, but their bellies are full and groaning.

The Iliad, xvi

The fury of war: Achilles in battle

He arms himself

Afterward he girt on about his chest the corselet,
and across his shoulders slung the sword with the nails of silver,
a bronze sword, and caught up the great shield, huge and heavy
next, and from it the light glimmered far, as from the moon.
And as when from across water a light shines to mariners
from a blazing fire, when the fire is burning high in the mountains
in a desolate steading, as the mariners are carried unwilling
by storm winds over the fish-swarming sea, far away from their
[loved ones;
so the light from the fair elaborate shield of Achilleus
shot into the high air. And lifting the helm he set it
massive upon his head, and the helmet crested with horse-hair
shone like a star, the golden fringes were shaken about it
which Hephaistos had driven close along the horn of the helmet.
And brilliant Achilleus tried himself in his armour, to see
if it fitted close, and how his glorious limbs ran within it,
and the armour became as wings and upheld the shepherd of the
[people.

The Iliad, xix

The massacre

As inhuman fire sweeps on in fury through the deep angles
of a drywood mountain and sets ablaze the depth of the timber
and the blustering wind lashes the flame along, so Achilleus
swept everywhere with his spear like something more than a
[mortal
harrying them as they died, and the black earth ran blood.
Or as when a man yokes male broad-foreheaded oxen
to crush white barley on a strong-laid threshing floor, and
[rapidly
the barley is stripped beneath the feet of the bellowing oxen,
so before great-hearted Achilleus the single-foot horses
trampled alike dead men and shields, and the axle under
the chariot was all splashed with blood and the rails which
[encircled

the chariot, struck by flying drops from the feet of the horses,
from the running rims of the wheels. The son of Peleus was
[straining
to win glory, his invincible hands spattered with bloody filth.

The Iliad, xx

Achilles and Lycaon

*Once already, Lycaon, son of Priam, had been taken by Achilles
and freed by ransom. But this time he pleads with his conqueror in
vain, and the latter reminds him that in war the law of death rules:*

'Poor fool, no longer speak to me of ransom, nor argue it.
In the time before Patroklos came to the day of his destiny
then it was the way of my heart's choice to be sparing
of the Trojans, and many I took alive and disposed of them.
Now there is not one who can escape death, if the gods send
him against my hands in front of Ilion, not one
of all the Trojans and beyond others the children of Priam.
So, friend, you die also. Why all this clamour about it?
Patroklos also is dead, who was better by far than you are.
Do you not see what a man I am, how huge, how splendid
and born of a great father, and the mother who bore me
[immortal?
Yet even I have also my death and my strong destiny,
and there shall be a dawn or an afternoon or a noontime
when some man in the fighting will take the life from me also
either with a spearcast or an arrow flown from the bowstring.'
So he spoke, and in the other the knees and the inward
heart went slack. He let go of the spear and sat back, spreading
wide both hands; but Achilleus drawing his sharp sword struck
[him
beside the neck at the collar-bone, and the double-edged sword
plunged full length inside. He dropped to the ground, face
[downward,
and lay at length, and the black blood flowed, and the ground
[was soaked with it.
Achilleus caught him by the foot and slung him into the river
to drift, and spoke winged words of vaunting derision over him:
'Lie there now among the fish, who will lick the blood away
from your wound, and care nothing for you, nor will your mother
lay you on the death-bed and mourn over you, but Skamandros
will carry you spinning down to the wide bend of the salt water.
And a fish will break a ripple shuddering dark on the water
as he rises to feed upon the shining fat of Lykaon.'

The Iliad, xxi

Achilles and the Scamander

The River, weary of the massacre Achilles is making on its banks, rushes against him, with all the power that it wields as a divinity.

And spear-famed Achilleus leapt into the middle water
with a spring from the bluff, but the river in a boiling surge was
[upon him
and rose making turbulent all his waters, and pushed off
the many dead men whom Achilleus had killed piled in
[abundance
in the stream; these, bellowing like a bull, he shoved out
on the dry land, but saved the living in the sweet waters
hiding them under the huge depths of the whirling current.
And about Achilleus in his confusion a dangerous wave rose
up, and beat against his shield and pushed it. He could not
brace himself with his feet, but caught with his hands at an
[elm tree
tall and strong grown, but this uptorn by the roots and tumbling
ripped away the whole cliff and with its dense tangle of roots
[stopped
the run of the lovely current and fallen full length in the water
dammed the very stream. Achilleus uprising out of the whirlpool
made a dash to get to the plain in the speed of his quick feet
in fear, but the great god would not let him be, but rose on him
in a darkening edge of water, minded to stop the labour
of brilliant Achilleus and fend destruction away from the Trojans.
The son of Peleus sprang away the length of a spearcast
running with the speed of the black eagle, the marauder
who is at once the strongest of flying things and the swiftest.
In the likeness of this he sped away, on his chest the bronze
[armour
clashed terribly, and bending away to escape from the river
he fled, but the river came streaming after him in huge noise.
And as a man running a channel from a spring of dark water
guides the run of the water among his plants and his gardens
with a mattock in his hand and knocks down the blocks in the
[channel;
in the rush of the water all the pebbles beneath are torn loose
from place, and the water that has been dripping suddenly jets on
in a steep place and goes too fast even for the man who guides it;
so always the crest of the river was overtaking Achilleus
for all his speed of foot, since gods are stronger than mortals.

The Iliad, xxi

Hera, fearing for Achilles, orders Hephaistos to stop the river with fire.

Hephaistos set on them an inhuman fire.
First he kindled a fire in the plain and burned the numerous
corpses that lay there in abundance, slain by Achilleus.
and all the plain was parched and the shining water was straitened.
As when the north wind of autumn suddenly makes dry
a garden freshly watered and makes glad the man who is
[tending it,
so the entire flat land was dried up with Hephaistos burning
the dead bodies. Then he turned his flame in its shining
into the river. The elms burned, the willows and tamarisks,
the clover burned and the rushes and the galingale, all those
plants that grew in abundance by the lovely stream of the river.
The eels were suffering and the fish in the whirl of the water
who leaped out along the lovely waters in every direction
in affliction under the hot blast of resourceful Hephaistos.
The strength of the river was burning away.

The Iliad, xxi

The death of Hector

The defeated Trojans have all returned within the walls save Hector.
Achilles, distracted for a moment by Apollo, whom he has pursued
in the form of Agenor, finally arrives beneath the walls.

The aged Priam was the first of all whose eyes saw him
as he swept across the flat land in full shining, like that star
which comes on in the autumn and whose conspicuous brightness
far outshines the stars that are numbered in the night's darkening,
the star they give the name of Orion's Dog, which is brightest
among the stars, and yet is wrought as a sign of evil
and brings on the great fever for unfortunate mortals.
Such was the flare of the bronze that girt his chest in his running.
The old man groaned aloud and with both hands high uplifted
beat his head, and groaned amain, and spoke supplicating
his beloved son, who there still in front of the gateway
stood fast in determined fury to fight with Achilleus.
The old man stretching his hands out called pitifully to him:
'Hektor, beloved child, do not wait the attack of this man
alone, away from the others. You might encounter your destiny
beaten down by Peleion, since he is far stronger than you are.
A hard man: I wish he were as beloved of the immortal
as loved by me. Soon he would lie dead, and the dogs and the
[vultures
would eat him, and bitter sorrow so be taken from my heart.

Oh, take

pity on me, the unfortunate still alive, still sentient
but ill-starred, whom the father, Kronos' son, on the threshold
[of old age
will blast with hard fate, after I have looked upon evils
and seen my sons destroyed and my daughters dragged away
[captive
and the chambers of marriage wrecked and the innocent children
[taken
and dashed to the ground in the hatefulness of war, and the wives
of my sons dragged off by the accursed hands of the Achaians.
And myself last of all, my dogs in front of my doorway
will rip me raw, after some man with stroke of the sharp bronze
spear, or with spearcast, has torn the life out of my body;
those dogs I raised in my halls to be at my table, to guard my
gates, who will lap my blood in the savagery of their anger
and then lie down in my courts. For a young man all is decorous
when he is cut down in battle and torn with the sharp bronze,
[and lies there
dead, and though dead still all that shows about him is beautiful;
but when an old man is dead and down, and the dogs mutilate
the grey head and the grey beard and the parts that are secret,
this, for all sad mortality, is the sight most pitiful.'
  So the old man spoke, and in his hands seizing the grey hairs
tore them from his head, but could not move the spirit in Hektor.
And side by side with him his mother in tears was mourning
and laid the fold of her bosom bare and with one hand held out
a breast, and wept her tears for him and called to him in winged
[words:
'Hektor, my child, look upon these and obey, and take pity
on me, if ever I gave you the breast to quiet your sorrow.
Remember all these things, dear child, and from inside the wall
beat off this grim man. Do not go out as champion against him,
o hard one; for if he kills you I can no longer
mourn you on the death-bed, sweet branch, o child of my bearing,
nor can your generous wife mourn you, but a big way from us
beside the ships of the Argives the running dogs will feed on
[you.'
  So these two in tears and with much supplication called out
to their dear son, but could not move the spirit in Hektor,
but he awaited Achilleus as he came on, gigantic.
But as a snake waits for a man by his hole, in the mountains,
glutted with evil poisons, and the fell venom has got inside him,
and coiled about the hole he stares malignant, so Hektor
would not give ground but kept unquenched the fury within him
and sloped his shining shield against the jut of the bastion.
Deeply troubled he spoke to his own great-hearted spirit.

The Iliad, xxii

Hector, speaking to himself, abandons the idea of making terms with Achilles.

So he pondered, waiting, but Achilleus was closing upon him
in the likeness of the lord of battles, the helm-shining warrior,
and shaking from above his shoulder the dangerous Pelian
ash spear, while the bronze that closed upon him was shining
like the flare of blazing fire or the sun in its rising.
And the shivers took hold of Hektor when he saw him, and
                                        [he could no longer
stand his ground there, but left the gates behind, and fled,
                                        [frightened,
and Peleus' son went after him in the confidence of his quick feet.
As when a hawk in the mountains who moves lightest of things
                                        [flying
makes his effortless swoop for a trembling dove, but she slips
                                        [away
from beneath and flies and he shrill screaming close after her
plunges for her again and again, heart furious to take her;
so Achilleus went straight for him in fury, but Hektor
fled away under the Trojan wall and moved his knees rapidly.
They raced along by the watching point and the windy fig tree
always away from under the wall and along the wagon-way
and came to the two sweet-running well springs. There there are
                                        [double
springs of water that jet up, the springs of whirling Skamandros.
One of these runs hot water and the steam on all sides
of it rises as if from a fire that was burning inside it.
But the other in the summer-time runs water that is like hail
or chill snow or ice that forms from water. Beside these
in this place, and close to them, are the washing-hollows
of stone, and magnificent, where the wives of the Trojans and
                                        [their lovely
daughters washed the clothes to shining, in the old days
when there was peace, before the coming of the sons of the
                                        [Achaians.
They ran beside these, one escaping, the other after him.
It was a great man who fled, but far better he who pursued him
rapidly, since here was no festal beast, no ox-hide
they strove for, for these are prizes that are given men for their
                                        [running.

                                        The Iliad, xxii

*Abandoned by the gods after the weighing of destinies, Hector is
distracted by Athena who assumes the features of his brother Deiphobus. He turns around, but after a double toss of spears to no
avail, he discovers that the false Deiphobus has disappeared. Yet
he speaks out.*

109

'Let me at least not die without a struggle, inglorious,
but do some big things first, that men to come shall know of it.'
    So he spoke, and pulling out the sharp sword that was slung
at the hollow of his side, huge and heavy, and gathering
himself together, he made his swoop, like a high-flown eagle
who launches himself out of the murk of the clouds on the flat
to catch away a tender lamb or a shivering hare; so   [land
Hektor made his swoop, swinging his sharp sword, and Achilleus
charged, the charge within him loaded with savage fury.
In front of his chest the beautiful elaborate great shield
covered him, and with the glittering helm with four horns
he nodded; the lovely golden fringes were shaken about it
which Hephaistos had driven close along the horn of the helmet.
And as a star moves among stars in the night's darkening,
Hesper, who is the fairest star who stands in the sky, such
was the shining from the pointed spear Achilleus was shaking
in his right hand with evil intention toward brilliant Hektor.
He was eyeing Hektor's splendid body, to see where it might best
give way, but all the rest of the skin was held in the armour,
brazen and splendid, he stripped when he cut down the strength
                                                        [of Patroklos;
yet showed where the collar-bones hold the neck from the
                                                        [shoulders,
the throat, where death of the soul comes most swiftly; in this
brilliant Achilleus drove the spear as he came on in fury,   [place
and clean through the soft part of the neck the spearpoint was
                                                        [driven.
Yet the ash spear heavy with bronze did not sever the windpipe,
so that Hektor could still make exchange of words spoken.
But he dropped in the dust, and brilliant Achilleus vaunted
                                                        [above him:
'Hektor, surely you thought as you killed Patroklos you would be
safe, and since I was far away you thought nothing of me,
o fool, for an avenger was left, far greater than he was,
behind him and away by the hollow ships. And it was I;
and I have broken your strength; on you the dogs and the vultures
shall feed and foully rip you; the Achaians will bury Patroklos.'
    In his weakness Hektor of the shining helm spoke to him:
'I entreat you, by your life, by your knees, by your parents,
do not let the dogs feed on me by the ships of the Achaians,
but take yourself the bronze and gold that are there in abundance,
those gifts that my father and the lady my mother will give you,
and give my body to be taken home again, so that the Trojans
and the wives of the Trojans may give me in death my rite of
                                                        .[burning.'
    But looking darkly at him swift-footed Achilleus answered:
'No more entreating of me, you dog, by knees or parents.

111

I wish only that my spirit and fury would drive me
to hack your meat away and eat it raw for the things that
you have done to me. So there is no one who can hold the
[dogs off
from your head, not if they bring here and set before me ten
[times
and twenty times the ransom, and promise more in addition,
not if Priam son of Dardanos should offer to weigh out
your bulk in gold; not even so shall the lady your mother
who herself bore you lay you on the death-bed and mourn you:
no, but the dogs and the birds will have you all for their feasting.'
   Then, dying, Hektor of the shining helmet spoke to him:
'I know you well as I look upon you, I know that I could not
persuade you, since indeed in your breast is a heart of iron.
Be careful now; for I might be made into the god's curse
upon you, on that day when Paris and Phoibos Apollo
destroy you in the Skaian gates, for all your valour.'
   He spoke, and as he spoke the end of death closed in upon him,
and the soul fluttering free of the limbs went down into Death's
[house
mourning her destiny, leaving youth and manhood behind her.
Now though he was a dead man brilliant Achilleus spoke to him:
'Die: and I will take my own death at whatever time
Zeus and the rest of the immortals choose to accomplish it.'
                                                    The Iliad, xxii

Pity: Priam before Achilles

Priam, led by the god Hermes, comes to plead with Achilles:

   ... Tall Priam
came in unseen by the other men and stood close beside him
and caught the knees of Achilleus in his arms, and kissed the
[hands
that were dangerous and manslaughtering and had killed so many
of his sons. As when dense disaster closes on one who has
[murdered
a man in his own land, and he comes to the country of others,
to a man of substance, and wonder seizes on those who behold
[him,
so Achilleus wondered as he looked on Priam, a godlike
man, and the rest of them wondered also, and looked at each
[other.
But now Priam spoke to him in the words of a suppliant:
'Achilleus like the gods, remember your father, one who
is of years like mine, and on the door-sill of sorrowful old age.

And they who dwell nearby encompass him and afflict him,
nor is there any to defend him against the wrath, the destruction.
Yet surely he, when he hears of you and that you are still living,
is gladdened within his heart and all his days he is hopeful
that he will see his beloved son come home from the Troad.
But for me, my destiny was evil. I have had the noblest
of sons in Troy, but I say not one of them is left to me.
Fifty were my sons, when the sons of the Achaians came here.
Nineteen were born to me from the womb of a single mother,
and other women bore the rest in my palace; and of these
violent Ares broke the strength in the knees of most of them,
but one was left me who guarded my city and people, that one
you killed a few days since as he fought in defence of his country,
Hektor; for whose sake I come now to the ships of the Achaians
to win him back from you, and I bring you gifts beyond number.
Honour then the gods, Achilleus, and take pity upon me
remembering your father, yet I am still more pitiful;
I have gone through what no other mortal on earth has gone
                                                            [through:
I put my lips to the hands of the man who has killed my children.'
   So he spoke, and stirred in the other a passion of grieving
for his own father. He took the old man's hand and pushed him
gently away, and the two remembered, as Priam sat huddled
at the feet of Achilleus and wept close for manslaughtering
and Achilleus wept now for his own father, now again   [Hektor
for Patroklos. The sound of their mourning moved in the house.
                                                            [Then
when great Achilleus had taken full satisfaction in sorrow
and the passion for it had gone from his mind and body,
                                                        [thereafter
he rose from his chair, and took the old man by the hand,
                                                        [and set him
on his feet again, in pity for the grey head and the grey beard.

                                                    The Iliad, xxiv

113

NOTES

1 André Gide, *Journal*. Pléiade edition, p. 1425, Oct. 25, 1938, and p. 238, Feb. 9, 1907.
2 In *laos* there is the root of our word *lay*, as in lay-brother; in Homer, the word opposes *man of the troops* to the great leaders, later the mass to the elite, and in Christian Greek, the non-clerics to the clergy.
3 The expression is Simone Weil's; but cf. Jean Wahl: *"Le monde d'Homère, c'est le monde de la force,"* preface to *On the Iliad*, by Rachel Bespaloff (New York, 1943); the latter also says (p. 18) "No one makes us more conscious of *the beauty of force* than Homer."
4 Book XXIV.
5 Book XXI.
6 Book I.
7 Book IX.
8 Book XVI.
9 This is where one can answer Péguy's remark that Homer's gods "lack all lack," "lack the final crown which is death's. And that consecration." (*Clio*, pp. 260 and 259 of the Pléiade edition.)
10 Péguy, op. cit. p. 248.
11 Book IX.
12 Book XVIII.
13 The cyclic poem (whether the word is taken in its exact sense or refers more widely to all imitations of Homer) is, according to Callimachus, the road everyone travels, the handsome boy who gives himself to all takers: that is, literary prostitution. (*Epigrams*, **XXVIII**).
14 The following lines from Book IX are those of a man who has morally suffered from the dissensions among the Hellenes:

Without tribe, without law, without home! the man
Who loves civil war makes one cold at heart.

15 *Pensées*, 303, 298, Brunschvicg edition.

16 Thus Menelaus in his deliberating monologue in Book XVIII.
17 See the episode of Lycaon translated above.
18 Book XX, Achilles at the massacre is *"mal'emmémaôs."*
19 As Zeus himself feels (Book XVIII).
20 Some excellent remarks on this subject are to be found in the *Homère* of Fernand Robert, chap. I, *"Le Merveilleux et l'expérience,"* as well as in E. R. Dodds' *The Greeks and the Irrational*, chap. I (Univ. of California Press, 1951).
21 Book II, 5-82. Nestor's suspicions imply that the false dream was already in Homer's time an oratorical artifice. The Orient preserves the practice.
22 Book V.
23 *Histoire Générale des Religions* (Gorce-Mortier), vol II, pp. 41-42.
24 *"Ein jeder Engel ist schrecklich,"* Rilke says: "Every angel is terrible" (Duino Elegies, 1, 7).
25 *Introduction à l'Iliade.*
26 The expression is that of P. Chantraine in the collective work *La Notion du Divin depuis Homère jusqu'à Platon*, p. 63 (*Entretiens sur l'Antiquité Classique*, vol. I [*Vandoeuvres-Genève, 1952*]. Fondation Hardt).
27 I am loosely translating the word *anamnesis* and the expression *ousia ontos ousa.*
28 Claudel, *Cinq Grandes Odes*, II, p. 64.
29 Book V.
30 Book IX.
31 Hermes has a curious remark on this, Book XXIV.
32 1 208b 30. I am indebted to Dodds' book, mentioned above, for the reference to this passage.
33 Book XV. *Kaka erga*, "acts which cause evil" rather than "bad actions" in terms of human morality; a declaration of fact rather than value judgment.
34 The same attachment to the other face of the Mother, to the Virgin, in the double defeat which Athena inflicts upon Ares; the same hostility to the brutal and, here, merely spear-carrying male; the humor of the second narrative need not cause it to be regarded as merely a comic incident.
35 Bassett's figures, *The Poetry of Homer*, p. 64.
36 W. Jaeger, *Paideia, the Ideals of Greek Culture*, vol. 1 (Oxford, 1946).
37 The expression is that of a Greek scholiast.
38 I refer my readers to the works of Gaston Bachelard in such matters.
39 Bassett, *op. cit.*, p. 168.
40 G. Bachelard, *La Terre et les rêveries du repos*, chap. IX.
41 Since 1700 at least, with Brendel; and the specialists have noted that there are never, in the *Iliad*, wounds anatomically impossible.
42 Certain epic characters were, perhaps, before Homer, minor local divinities (though it is difficult to find proof of this in so remote a time, and though one should suspect, for all evidence posterior to the epic, the tendency of antiquity to "rediscover" in the past more recent legends). But in Homer's text, even sons of gods are only men.
43 See my *Homère et la mystique des Nombres*, pp. 75-77.
44 M. L. Sjoestedt, *Dieux et heros des Caltes*, pp. 85-86.
45 The old translation "shameful portions" is ridiculous to the ancient Greek mind, and even to that of the Old Testament, some of whose texts bear witness to oaths sworn on these organs.

THE ODYSSEY, OR THE SOUL'S WEDDING

The *Odyssey* "remains the oldest book worth reading for the
story it tells, and the first European novel." This is the judgment
of T. E. Lawrence, after translating the poem and weighing
its author's weaknesses without too much sympathy.[1] And it is
true that its novelistic side, its nursery tales make it much
easier to get into than *The Iliad*. Very little need be pruned
from its central section (Ulysses' adventures in distant seas on
the way home from Troy) to keep a young audience breathless;
both cuts and preparation are necessary to present the great
episodes of *The Iliad* to a similar audience. Many grown-up
readers react in the same way.

Certainly violent death is as rampant, at times, as beneath
the walls of Troy; more unrestricted in one sense: Ulysses
returns alone, all his crew has perished; in the final slaughter
not one suitor escapes. But these sailors were only silhouettes,
with neither name nor face, to whom it was impossible to
become attached.[2] Many of the suitors are no more distinct,
and what we can guess of their character does not make us
mourn them. We do not smell the odor of corpses everywhere,
to the point of obsession. And there remain long hours of
fragrance: the woods and pastures of Ithaca, the city of the
Phaeacians, the isles of the goddesses, the sea.

119

The shores of Corfu

The poem's defect is an occasional lack of dramatic tension, particularly in the travels of Telemachus and in Ulysses' sojourn with his old swineherd Eumaeus. Except for the central section, with its stories of heroes which refer to a period nine years earlier, *The Odyssey* is no longer the continuous cinema constantly furnishing visual images in a direct line of action. The composition is already that of a novelistic narrative: we follow one character, then another; even within a single Book, the scene may change. These jumps occasionally offer certain difficulties to the exegete who attempts to draw up an exact calendar of events: adjustments in continuity were not the poet's first concern. The reader scarcely notices such difficulties, but if he enjoys being swept on to the final catastrophe by a violent and rapid movement, he is justified in feeling that certain pauses are too long. Besides, the poem reserves its catastrophes only for the "bad people," and once Penelope has recognized her husband, its action, for us, is complete. Nevertheless, the narrative continues for still another Book (some of its contents are not authentic, but not everything in it must be condemned too quickly). This ending tends to be wearisome.

To keep up with *The Iliad's* high pitch over a single prolonged reading is not easy. *The Odyssey* is a work we can pick up and lay down with greater ease. It falls, moreover, into natural sections: Telemachus' Travels (Books I to IV); the Return of Ulysses, as far as Phaeacia (Books V to VIII); the long Story of his Adventures he tells there (Books IX to XII); his Arrival in Ithaca and Homecoming (Books XIII to XX); the Slaughter of the Suitors and the Recognition Scene (Books XXI to XXIII). None is self-sufficient, for all are arranged with a view to the conclusion; but if we space out our reading, there is no difficulty recovering the desired tone. Not that *The Odyssey* fails to possess the moments of involvement characteristic of its sister epic. But it functions by other spells, other, less extreme charms: its storms and its monsters do not weigh so heavily upon the reader, probably because the story-teller is tired of the former, and does not really believe in the latter. His lack of faith creates a distance between us and the action. On the other hand the author of *The Iliad*, even when he adds a word of personal commentary, is a witness at our side; we live several days of the Trojan War with him. We are less continually beside Ulysses.

Athena

Faces of The Odyssey

In *The Iliad,* everything was on the level of human experience for its author, even the comings and goings of the gods. I do not know whether he actually *saw* them himself,[3] but he knew how to recognize them; and to imagine the heroes, he drew on tradition, the excellence of which he never doubted, and on his own instinct of greatness. In *The Odyssey,* however, tradition and the supernatural occupy an entirely different place.

Naturally Homer retains from the epic repertory the character of Ulysses, with certain personality traits, the name of his son and his father (though Penelope is not mentioned in *The Iliad*). Menelaus, Helen, Nestor, Agamemnon, Ajax, Achilles, the greatest heroes reappear briefly in the poem; but only the first three are still alive. The author also chooses to recall, as a contrast to the faithful couple, the misfortunes of Agamemnon and Clytemnestra. But the court of Sparta, and still less that of Pylos, are not on a plane with those of Alcinous and Arete, sovereigns of the Phaeacians and strangers to the tradition of Troy. The Great War itself is referred to in many places, but the only episode developed from it at some length is treated by Ulysses himself in the spirit of a mere soldier, no longer that of a hero, and with apparent humor. There are only a few distant fires to remind us of an event from which the traveler has grown somewhat detached, with no sense of return: the focus is on the sea, and on Ithaca.

For the gods too, the bard must seek elsewhere besides the tradition. Poseidon and Athene clash over Ulysses' return, but their conflict does not put them directly at grips with each other, even in verbal dispute. The goddess especially fails her protégé during the more tragic portion of his adventures. There are explanations to be made for this absence,[4] but its result is that the hero is alone in victory as in

Poseidon

anguish, and that having borne all danger, he assumes all glory. Since the great gods prefer to remain in Olympus, it is the secondary "powers" attached to distant islands who undertake the direction of affairs, to protect Ulysses but also to keep him from going on: Circe, borrowed from the legend of the Argonauts; Calypso, daughter of Atlas. These women, the first of whom is drawn in bolder relief with witchlike attributes, appeal to the imagination; but they were at no time the object of a cult; they do not touch the hearts of pious listeners like the Lady of the nearby temple.

The poet's great stroke of audacity has been to take Ulysses to the confines of the land of the Dead and to raise up the Shades (by highly unorthodox necromantic rites). And it is of little consequence that Tiresias' revelations, which he has come to hear, furnish nothing startling: the effect remains a powerful one. But what are the elements on which its emotional impression rests? The eternal shadow that falls across these desolate shores; the blood of the sacrifice which the Shades drink in order to recover a little spiritual life; the horror felt by a people nourished on light for the dreadful condition of the weak souls lost in the darkness; the most visceral dread, "green fear" at the thought that Persephone might turn the petrifying head of the Gorgon against the intruders. And the same ele-

124

Ulysses at Circes' Palace (British Museum)

mental terror runs down our spines when we accompany Ulysses into the Cyclops' cave. From the marvellous Uranian, the butt of the gods of light, we move on to the fantasy of ogres, wizards, deep-sea monsters, ghosts.

All of Ulysses' adventures in distant lands are derived from folklore. Methodical analysis has disclosed corrupted myths, rituals whose meaning has been lost (particularly initiation rites), and, just as often, magical practices still extant.[5] Through the distorting mediums which have made them into popular traditions, the written texts of the Ancient East, actual literary works (the Babylonian epic of Gilgamesh, the story of the Egyptian shipwreck) have doubtless helped shape the action. Long before Homer, descents among the Dead were classic themes of religious thought in Asia Minor and Egypt.[6] There is a long, ancient past which funnels into the Greek imagination. It is impossible to date, even approximately, but we recognize in it the layers of successive civilizations: hunters' rites, then shepherds', ceremonies connected with the cultivation of grain, bronze smelters' magic, royal traditions linked to archery, navigation on rafts built according to Egyptian techniques.

Yet it is not only the prehistory of Hellenic thought which is affected by these contributions. By employing themes and images which have haunted the human imagination for thousands of years, the poet has found, in his listeners' hearts, roads which the heroic epic had never traveled. The cavern, the solitary house in the heart of the forest, the woman with secret powers who rules over wild beasts, the lost island where love endures impervious to time: the themes have continued down through the ages, always recognizable, in forever new guises – to be proposed to young imaginations with unfailing success. Here are many of the "archetypes" which rule our dreams and our barely conscious fabulations. When the bard gives himself up to the joy of story-telling, he assures his text a high fantasy "charge," more universal, more readily renewed, than the warrior pathos of *The Iliad*.

But, either to obtain periods of emotional relief or because he is not convinced enough to let himself go for long, the bard alternates such fully developed episodes as the adventure in Polyphemus' cave or the sojourn on Circe's island with sketches that are hardly more than diagrams. Certain narratives, thus reduced, fall into obscurities difficult to resolve, or wind up as mutilated fables [7] which only our knowledge of folklore permits us to reconstitute. This accentuates the impression that Homer, not as close to his subject at every point as he was in *The Iliad*, does not have it under the same control. From every evidence, he would not have enriched his narrative with foreign tales (wherever he found them) if he had not had a weakness for them, but the genius of his race often carries him away. It is on Ionian soil, in contact with the Orient, that the Greek people begins to philosophize; but its philosophy, reduced to the level of the average Hellene, is a certain taste for the "reasonable" acquired without effort, rather than for the rational won at the cost of rigorous thinking. Common sense does not sort well with the fantastic – nor, on the other side, any better with science.

Its diversity occasionally gives *The Odyssey* the quality of an *enjoyable novel*, and this adjective is the last one would dream of applying at any point to *The Iliad*. We are not far, either, from the sentimental novel. Not only because there are many tears, and for less urgent reasons than in *The Iliad*, but because certain central or episodic themes play on emotions easy to arouse and which the tradition of the novel has tirelessly exploited: the dog faithful to its master when men have forgotten him and who dies when he is found again, the hidden hero hearing his own exploits recalled, the master of the house turned away from his own door as a beggar, the shipwrecked man secretly returning to his country apprehensive that his wife has remarried, the wife incredulous before her husband when everyone else has already recognized him.

To the adjective "sentimental," late eighteenth century usage added that of *virtuous*. *The Odyssey* is also a *virtuous* novel. Ulysses prefers his wife to the immortality Calypso would give him; Laertes has not touched his servant girl Euryclea in order not to distress the queen; young Telemachus apparently has no "escapades"; Nausicaa, Arete, Penelope, Helen herself are models of the virtuous woman at various ages; the servant girls who connived with the suitors are punished, even with ignominious death. *The Odyssey* glorifies conjugal love. Ulysses' romances with Circe or Calypso are not contradictions: these goddesses are not women. It would be indiscreet to confuse these unions, which are divine favors, with the adventures of a sailor on shore leave; they belong, for the ancient, to another order.

By pointing out all the past *The Odyssey* has behind it, and all the future it prefigures, we may see more clearly what it is *not*. The idea that it might conceal (strange riddle!) a precise geographical science or serve as an artful vehicle for nautical instructions, whether Phoenician or otherwise, could occur only to minds more accustomed to the ingenuities of erudition than to poetic creation. What notion can such minds have of a poet and his work? Besides, how can one take seriously the "location" of Odyssean sites which shift from place to place at the whim of the interpreters, and which can often be decided only by forcing or forgetting the text? Who is being fooled, for instance, when Circe's island, plainly situated in the East of the world, in the open sea, is identified as an Italian peninsula? The poet has had Ulysses forced out of the real world by a long tempest, has set him on a magic ship, passing through a dream country which a god may since have destroyed. In other words, he has taken pains to warn us that he has permitted himself every liberty and has happily exempted us from considering any real place. What dreadful constraints we would force upon him! And for what results! What light could geographical hypotheses shed on the poem as poem, on every-

127

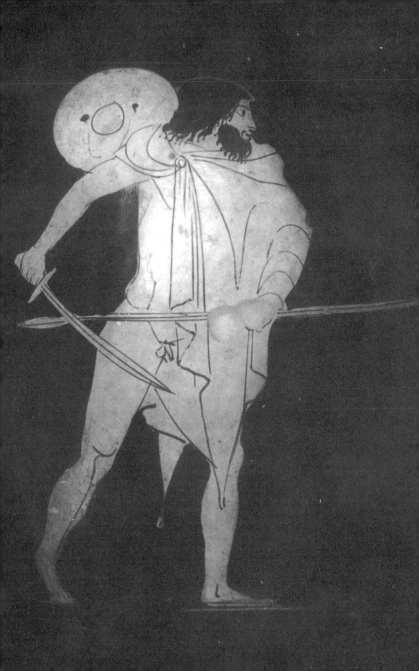

thing which constitutes the *raison d'etre* of the work and which assures its survival?

Considering the central position which the Journey to the Shades occupies in *The Odyssey*, one might feel much more tempted to discover in this epic a poem of initiation, an itinerary of the soul that dies and is reborn. But, presented rigorously to explain *everything* in the action, this hypothesis would be unwarranted. Ulysses does not seek the last word about the human condition from the dead; more prosaically, he wants to know if he can get back home, and how. We should prefer him to manifest a deeper curiosity, but we are not rewriting the poem: it remains what it is, the work of an imaginative man, not a mystic.

Not that we must entirely reject the notion that *The Odyssey* contains a lesson. But it is simple and immediate. The life of Ulysses bears its own moral: he has survived by dint of patience, and thanks to the faculty of resourcefulness in meeting circumstance which the Greeks, call *metis*, a virtue abundantly attributed to him by a poetic formula. Not for nothing is he the protégé of Athena, who incarnates divine *metis*. It is unfortunate that a tradition which begins with the Greek tragedians has given Ulysses the reputation of being a nasty cheat. In *The Odyssey* he employs deception only in self-defense and no one dreams of reproaching him for it. Ruse is an indispensable weapon in societies where the untempered exercise of frankness immediately ruins anyone so foolish as to give himself up to it. This is still true today in countries where, since the world began, nothing protects the individual against despotism or anarchy.[8]

The gods do not consider that the ruses of Ulysses diminish his merits. Ulysses has always respected them. If he has blinded Polyphemus, Poseidon's son, to escape from a desperate situation, he was ignorant of this relationship, whereas his crew knew he was committing a sacrilege by eating the oxen of the Sun. Therefore the sailors perished, while their leader finally manages to appease the god of the waves. *The Odyssey* advises piety in all its forms, including respect for the poor.

Ulysses was early interpreted by the Greek moralists as a model of temperance in the strongest sense of the word. Prudence and temperance: two cardinal virtues in his favor. Strength of soul: a third. As for justice, according to the rude concepts of a time when the sword was held in higher esteem,

Ulysses is not lacking in this virtue either. And if we cannot grant him hope in the "theological" sense of the term, unknown in the ancient world, we must at least admit that he bears solidly pinned to his intrepid body and soul the expectation of his final return. The Mediterranean will-to-live, clinging to existence whatever happens? Undoubtedly, but whether tied to a wreck or cast upon a rock, Ulysses *thinks*; it is not a blind instinct that leads him and saves him, it is an enlightened will.

Certainly the poet has embodied in his hero the human examples observed around him, but if he has been able to combine them into an eternal type, it is because he carried in himself a certain idea of the complete man. By imposing it upon his hearers as an image, he oriented their profound desires much more powerfully than by versifying moral maxims.

The paradise of the mother

At the moment Ulysses' return begins, the tenth year after the fall of Troy, the Achaean lands have emerged from the post-war difficulties. At Ithaca, the suitors clustered for three years around Penelope bring ruin to the palace and trouble to the island, but at least they have not shed human blood, and the listener hardly takes seriously their plot to assassinate Telemachus. All the action which occurs in the real world presents the image of a society again at peace, and it is not surprising that its life has an altogether different savor from that beneath the walls of Ilium. It is the return of the "old soldier" and his desire for vengeance which bring Force and Death back on the stage.

As long as he wandered the seas, Ulysses and his men still formed, as at Troy, a society of men, adapted to war. Actually, in this "poem of the sea," the time spent on the waves is quite short – less than two years. It is enough, however, for Ulysses and his sailors to be subjected to powers outside the human order, against which unaided human strength cannot prevail: giants like the Cyclops and the Lestrygonians, monsters like Scylla and Charybdis, magicians and supernatural figures like Aeolus, Circe, the Sirens. Spear and sword are useless against them, as Ulysses discovers with Scylla. It is no longer a question of facing an honorable death in equal combat, of receiving, if vanquished, a burial according to the rites, but of being felled like an ox or swallowed alive. Such a fate is

131

hardly preferable to being turned into an animal with a touch of a wand or into stone on Hades' threshold; not to mention death at sea, abandoning the corpse to the fish. Confronting these destinies, the soul of ancient man is gripped by a shudder of profound revulsion such as war does not inspire in him. Ulysses' struggles put him with the Argonauts and the great killers of monsters, no longer with the heroes of Troy.

These are reasons why *The Odyssey* describes, in its conflicts as in peace, a world unlike that of *The Iliad*. But under these basic conditions, nothing necessitated the predominance of women, which the author delights in translating into images throughout the entire work. Women who dominate, in fact, in two ways: in the poem, they exercise (and not only on the hero) an uncontested influence; in the memory of the listeners, they establish themselves with as much or more vitality than the men who surround them, with the exception of Ulysses.

Let us name them. Penelope, whose appearance always electrifies the suitors, even when the ruse of the loom has been discovered, and from whom Ulysses himself, after the triumph, awaits consent to join her in the conjugal chamber. Helen, who rules in Lacedaemon like "Artemis of the Golden Shaft" (yes, like the goddess of chastity) and who offers Telemachus a veil she has embroidered with her own hands as a gift for his future wife. Nausicaa, who has already inherited from her mother the queenly self-possession, decision, and grandeur that effortlessly gets its way. It is to her mother Arete, who sits among the Phaeacian leaders beside her husband the king, that Ulysses' first words are addressed when he seeks asylum, following the advice of the goddess who protects him. Need we mention Circe – an immortal – who enslaves in animal form all the men who approach her? With her, and for the first time in literature, as far as we know, we enter a strictly feminine society. She lives, of course, withdrawn from the world, on an island, like Calypso. The latter is apparently alone, unless her "house" is not simply a euphemism. Ulysses has never been more dependent on a feminine whim than with these two goddesses, since he cannot leave either without her consent, without the favorable winds she can give him, nor find the way without her detailed instructions.

Woman as queen, as jailer and liberator, woman as counselor. And the most active Olympian divinity in the poem, the one who, acting as a comrade, helps Ulysses conceal his

132

treasures, is the Wise Virgin, Athena; no longer the rough warrior maid of *The Iliad* but the sly girl who amuses herself by tricking her protégé when he thinks he is at his most cunning. Ranged from earth all the way to Olympus, a series of feminine figures, benevolent and circumspect, illuminates the poem and guides the hero or his son. We must wait for the *Divina Commedia* to find again this combination of a man hard-pressed by life, thirsting for revenge, and a young female genius who takes him by the hand. But Beatrice leads the soul to beatific vision, while Athena, in the form of a swallow, looks on at the final massacre which she has desired more ardently than Ulysses himself. The Greek gods do not give their pity to everyone!

In a view based on the mural paintings of Minoan Crete and the Mycenae which bear witness to the participation of women in spectacles and ceremonies and, in Crete, their predominant sacerdotal role, *The Odyssey* has been interpreted as a reminiscence of these remote centuries. It is very likely, as a matter of fact, that such striking characteristics of long vanished societies should remain etched in the popular memory. Furthermore, the folklore from which the bard borrowed so heavily was particularly suited to furnish him, from widely varying sources, images, of sorceresses and initiating priestesses. Now with the "archetypes" folklore provides, we gain access to the secret layers of inner life. When a poet unceasingly returns to the same images, it is because they haunt the obscure regions where his imagination is nourished. Homer is under the influence of the Mother, in the psychoanalytic and religious senses of the word (both senses are closely intertwined, but the more fundamental is perhaps the second: The Oedipus legend, for instance, may be a "recent" Hellenic corruption of the hierogamy of the king and the Mother Goddess, to which the taint of incest was added only later by narrow-minded men). In *The Odyssey* we recognize much more powerfully than in *The Iliad* the age-old attachment of the Aegeans to the multiple and complementary figures of the Great Goddess, sometimes Mother and Wife, sometimes the severe Virgin who punishes a mere glance with death, sometimes the sacred Prostitute consecrated to carnal love.

What assures *The Odyssey* its magnificent equilibrium is the emphatically male character of its hero. Were he less strongly tried, less robust in body and soul, less assured, less aggressive, Ulysses would not counterbalance the feminity of the poem virtually single handed. The triple union of the hero with Circe, with Calypso, and finallly with his recovered wife re-establishes this harmony of the sexes, which is fundamentally an expression of cosmic harmony. Better still, Homer, in honor of the royal couple, has the coming of Dawn postponed by Athena herself. So it is the Virgin who by this miracle conse-crates the triumph of conjugal love and, as we would say today, sanctifies it.

Thus the soul, plunged by a simple reading into the deep current of the poem, issues, gradually purged of its nightmares and its passions, out into sunlight again. At the end of *The Iliad*, on the contrary, it did not emerge from the circle of violence save for a brief truce. If *The Odyssey* leads to an inner completion like the *Divina Commedia,* it is because the two poems trace the two surest ways open to the human person for the achievement of a well-founded equilibrium: the one more accessible: marriage, taken in its sacred significance; the other reserved to redeemed souls: the contemplative union with God.

Of course no reader should assume that Homer consciously calculated such an effect. He has let himself be guided (wisdom

135

or nonchalance?) by the great images which filled his dreams; he has remained faithful. in short, to the fables of his childhood and his adolescence.

I see further evidence of this idealistic youth in the sketch of several utopian societies Ulysses encounters in his travels. The lotus of oblivion, the island floating on walls of bronze, the bard owed these to folklore. But popular tales do not invent types of societies. Yet if we take the Lotus-eaters, who receive the Achaeans with gifts of the "honey-sweet" fruit of forgetfulness, or Aeolus and his children who spend their lives feasting, or even the Cyclops, who do not appear to deserve such happiness, we find human groups whose life does not seem to require effort, the first two spontaneously hospitable. The poet has enjoyed himself describing the anarchy of the Cyclops: no laws, no *agora* for public discussion; an authority strictly familial; each creature rules over his own tribe in his own cave; no tilling the soil, for the vines and the wheat grow by themselves; nothing but the care of the herds. The Phaecians, with their looms and their shipbuilding, belong more to the real world. But their souls have retained a primitive purity, since the gods like to come familiarly among them. An optimistic soul is expressing itself in such dreams, preferring smiling faces and long conversations to continuous labor. And here *The Odyssey*, with its *"bons sauvages"* anticipates the *Bougainville's Travels* aspect of the eighteenth century.

Even on Ithaca, a relatively poor island, life would be idyllic without the harassment of the suitors. It had been so, at least for those who knew how to live humanely. Eumaeus' remarks show how Homer conceives relations between the just master, the generous mistress of the house, and the slave raised in the family. Of course there are bad servants in Ithaca, and a contemptible beggar; but they could never have manifested their real nature had it not been for the master's absence.

Thus, despite a subject which does not spare us its scenes of horror, the poet escapes whenever possible to places where the good life is lived. His heart is so little on the battlefields that once he reaches the final slaughter, instead of *seeing* it and describing it as he sees it, he takes refuge, at least for hand-to-hand struggles, in a whole series of formulas familiar from *The Iliad*. His account does not make us tremble a moment, despite a few reversals, for the three faithful servants who fight at Ulysses' side. He has not been willing to kill off a

Ulysses disguised as a beggar before Penelope (Louvre)

single one of them out of respect for realism; even to inflict some serious wound. He is too good-hearted to hurt such sympathetic characters.

Divine clemency and future life

His gods are not unlike him. A cowherd (and therefore a slave) can remind us, in the pure tradition of *The Iliad*, that no divinity is so much a *god of destruction* as Zeus and that *he has no pity for men*, that he has created them *to plunge them into misery;* [9] as a matter of fact, in contradiction to these remarks is the thought Zeus himself formulates at the very beginning of *The Odyssey* with reference to Priam's affirmation that *the gods are the cause* and not Helen:

137

> Alas, how these mortals accuse the gods of all their woes!
> From us, to hear them, come their troubles; and it is they them-
> [selves,
> Distracted with pride, who make each other suffer beyond the
> measure of fate.

This is already the notion for which Plato will find the lapidary formula: *theos anaitios*, "God is not responsible." [10] While in *The Iliad* the word *hybris* had not yet acquired the sense of "excess," here it has this nuance, fundamental to the moral thought of classical Greece, and applied to the exactions of the suitors. It is the latter in particular, in the poem, who will suffer – to the point of destruction – the consequences of their wicked actions and even to the same extent, of their intentions.

The text frequently reminds us that the gods punish crime, but it sometimes manages, at the same time, to declare that they recompense the justice and good actions of men. The poet goes further: both Zeus, invoked as *hiketesios* or *xeinios*, and the gods in general, the divine powers, keep particular watch over the suppliants, the beggars, the poor, the wanderers and foreigners. It is Eumaeus, the swineherd, who declares as much to his errant master:

> It would be a sin for me, stranger (were one poorer than you to
> [come
> Not to house a guest. They are all from Zeus,
> Guests and beggars. [11]

Ulysses, struck by the young Antinous, threatens him with the Erinyes, who also exist for the poor. [12] In both cases, those who throw themselves on divine mercy are, or seem to be, dis-inherited, and we sympathize with their impulse, but Antinous, enraged as he is, does not contest Ulysses' remarks, and an-other suitor even adds this remark, which has a new sound:

> Striking this unhappy waif was a sin, Antinous, which will seal your fate so surely as there is a God in heaven. Not to mention that these very Gods are always disguising themselves as travellers from abroad and roaming our settlements to note human good or ill.
>
> *The Odyssey*, xvii

The old notion that a god may be hidden in mortal guise

138

assumes a moral value here. The gods no longer disguise themselves to aid a friend or deceive an enemy. Now they are defenders of a moral law left unspecified but which the bard would probably tell us could be found in moderate minds. Curiously, the gods resemble, in their "tours of inspection," the angels of the Old Testament.

It becomes possible to trust not only the divinity known to be one's protector, but the gods in general. To his old nurse, who has just recognized him, Ulysses declares: "Keep my words in silence, and turn to the gods."

Athena herself tells him as much: Instead of confiding in some friend who is only a mortal *and who has not so many ideas*, it would be better to rely on the gods.[13]

The bard has not ignored the classical objection; it is not always apparent that the gods punish crime. But, he replies, even during a successful raid pirates feel in their hearts the terrible power of dread; the wicked man is cursed in his lifetime and despised after his death, while the virtuous man enjoys a good reputation. It is therefore the better policy always to act virtuously: it is his *euergesie*, his "good behavior," which has saved the herald Medon from the general slaughter. And though such remarks doubtless lead us into marketplace optimism, let us recall how Achilles triumphed over the dying Hector, and then remember Ulysses' gesture, when before the heaped corpses old Euryclea wants to raise the ritual cry of victory; he stops her and exclaims:

Old woman, keep your joy for yourself, be still, raise no shout!
God forbids raising the shout of victory over men one has slain.
It is fate, the work of the gods, which has conquered these; and
[it is their crime.

If the bard makes his contemporaries deeply aware of this restraint, we can pardon him an occasional moment of preachifying.

Yet we must not, on the other hand, make *The Odyssey* sound tamer than it is: though he has spared the life of only two honest men who have fallen among the suitors, the bard (of course) and the herald, Ulysses, thirty lines further will have twelve servant girls executed and coldly mutilated before putting the treacherous goatherd to death. Telemachus, rivaling him (in what seems to be his first combat), hangs the wretched girls whom his father had destined for the sword, so that they will not have a "proper" death. Men are not tender-hearted when they believe they are rightfully executing divine vengeance: they bear a terrible resemblance to those who pursue a personal *vendetta*.

In Book XI, *The Odyssey* paints a terrible picture of the world of the Dead. All that remains of man is a phantom which reproduces his features, but which no longer has the faculty of thought; it retains just enough sensitivity to suffer. A twilight of the soul in a nocturnal landscape. But recall Book IV: Proteus prophesies to Menelaus a happy survival in Elysium, a land without winter, eternally refreshed by Zephyr. The two views are not necessarily contradictory: On the one side would be the immense number of ordinary shades, and on the other a few elect. It is possible, too, that the bard, drawing on two traditions of different origin, has juxtaposed them without bothering to set them in agreement. The fact remains that the notion of election remains implicit; it is not explained why Menelaus should be promised this condition while Achilles or the soothsayer Tiresias is excluded from it.[14] Certainly Menelaus is not recommended by any eminent virtue. It would therefore be unwise to suppose that there exists in the author's mind a necessary relation between eternal felicity and the merits of the elect. Otherwise, would he not promise such felicity to encourage men to virtue?

His optimism, apparently, does not smile for long in questions of future life. If *The Odyssey* is the poem of tenacious will finally recompensed, it is not a poem of divine hope as a worshipper of Demeter might have celebrated it.

Discovery of tense and person

If, on the whole, the tone of *The Odyssey* is not profoundly tragic in quality like *The Iliad*, if its progress is more that of a novel, still its dramatic element is no less abundant. The struggles are given less violent expression, but are waged with just as much intensity. The spoken portions, according to statistics, occupy fifty-four per cent of the poem, a proportion apparently higher than that noted for the other epic, though this indication is false, for we must deduct the stories Ulysses tells in Alcinous' court, at least when he is not quoting con-versations. If they are spoken, this is only a device of nar-

140

ration – and besides, it was a stroke of genius to have the hero himself recount his strangest adventures. In any case, there is a great deal of talking in *The Odyssey*, and, as always in Greece, it is done naturally and skillfully.

I called Ulysses' narratives a stroke of genius. In *The Iliad*, a character may describe an episode in his life; but, unless his name is Nestor, he goes directly to the essentials, compressing the years into a few lines. And even Nestor cannot yield too long to the inclinations of old age, or he would interrupt the action. Homer, by making first-person narration an essential element of his work, has opened up an infinite future in time and space by this device. Its success has still not been exhausted. As for his characters, he has achieved two results. First of all, by referring us ten years back, making us pass over or glimpse the intervening years, he has put his characters at grips with time; then, by identifying the hero's voice with his own Books, he has granted Ulysses a "presence" which no other figure of either epic attains.

Actually, we may think that time passes over the heroes of the poem without affecting them. This is true of Menelaus and of Helen, of Ulysses and Penelope in their physical appearance; we are never told that they have aged. This is a vestige of the mentality of popular legends and really archaic tales. The bard, more conscious, finds himself hampered by this tradition. Fortunately, to return home as an old beggar, Ulysses needs his divine protectress to transform his very flesh; it is not difficult, afterwards, to restore it to its orginal beauty. Penelope likes to say she has lost all her "bloom" since her husband's departure; at least, she has wept a great deal. The same goddess therefore rejuvenates her appearance so that she may look to her best advantage before the gathered suitors. Thus the poet takes his precautions against skeptical hearers.

The fact remains, nevertheless, that time, to penetrate human beings, has one powerful weapon at its disposal: grief. Anticleis, Ulysses' mother, has died of it, and Laertes, his old father, is about to. Ulysses is so tough that everything wears out against his patience, but the callosity produced by his trials has certainly helped thicken his natural armor. This is the mark the years have left upon him. Penelope, for her part, owes, as much to the years as to her native caution, her unconquerable suspicion which causes her to hesitate for so long in recognizing the wanderer. In any case, in these elite natures, time spoils nothing. They become concentrated, tougher; and, faithful to their inner imperatives, they survive. A modern reader is tempted not to believe in such perseverance. Is this not because he rarely encounters people so endowed with *life?* But among peoples who have remained close to nature, they can still be met today.

This was probably the first time, not only in Greece, but in all ancient literature, that an author put his creatures at grips with time. We must therefore admire how Homer has been able to represent, alongside his "hardened" characters, those whose features time has not yet molded. For it is he who has created *the* young man and *the* young girl, Telemachus and Nausicaa. In *The Iliad*, we know Achilles is the youngest of the Greek heroes, but whatever his age, his mind is adult. We need not discuss Nausicaa, who has always enchanted the critics. If, on the other hand, Telemachus has often been misinterpreted, it is because the vagueness of his character derives precisely from the fact that he is *the* young man.

From adolescence, he has retained a mixture of fear and respect with regard to an old king as venerable as Nestor: he hesitates to question him, taking refuge in his inexperience in the art of speaking.[15] Even after his return from Lacedaemonia, when the reception and the gifts Menelaus has bestowed assure him, in his own people's eyes, of that position which, today, diplomatic recognition confers on a government, he feels uncertain of his authority. This is why, from time to time, he adopts a cutting tone and a certain brutality in order to put the suitors in their place. These are the timid man's fits of energy.

At home, he is surrounded by anxious affection, as much from his mother as from old Euryclea. Therefore, on his return from Sparta, he rather dryly interrupts his mother's tears, using the greeting of a guest as an excuse: he is afraid to show his feelings. He manages to send her back to her womanly occupations without amenity. This is the touchy side of youth importuned by too much love. But the same Telemachus will "recognize" the father he has never seen, for no better reason than an impulse of spontaneous emotion. Despite his apprehensions, he follows him in the unequal struggle which he must undertake, always trusting his wisdom. The last words he speaks, during the recognition scene between husband and wife, after having rebelled against his mother's incredulity, are

once more to express his reliance on this tested wisdom.

In the trial of the bow, he alone might have succeeded in bending his father's weapon had the latter not stopped him with a sign. This is a way of making it known that he has actually reached his majority and that he will be the worthy heir of Ulysses. His travels, this struggle, have matured him. Of course *The Odyssey* is a good deal more than a prince's *Bildungsroman*, but by displaying this irreproachable young man in a discreet antithesis to the unfortunate Orestes, his author has prepared the way for Fénelon. He proposes a model, if not a pedagogy.

The patina the years have left on Ulysses' face, the sound of his voice, heard only at the most striking moments of the poem, are certainly two of the most important advantages among all those he enjoys over the other Homeric characters, even over Helen. The human mind turns back to him across the centuries, as to one of the great figures in which our dreams are made flesh.[16] Whether he is reincarnated in works of pure imagination or whether his person serves as a focus for broad reflections on man, particularly on Mediterranean man,[17] Ulysses is with us. In our heart, in our acts. The rafts we launch upon the immensities of the Pacific these days reproduce that of Ulysses, through models borrowed from Peru and Polynesia.[18] Our solitary navigators have their heart fixed like the hero of the tempests. We no longer fight like Achilles; but a shipwrecked man on a raft is still Ulysses.

The poet and his inner landscape

Storm and shipwreck: there is one character in *The Odyssey* without equivalent in *The Iliad*, and that is the sea. We need not give this figure more attention than it demands: it is virtually absent from the second half of the poem as from the first two Books. No pursuits on the high seas, no grapplings or collisions; furthermore, the ancient navigator, surprised by a storm, had no other resource than to let himself be carried before it. Nothing about life on board: in practice, every effort was made to spend only the daylight hours at sea. Few "seascapes"; Homer of *The Iliad*, gifted with a more powerful gaze, paints them better. And, of course, no love for the sea and the beings inhabiting it: the author of *The Odyssey* loathes

145

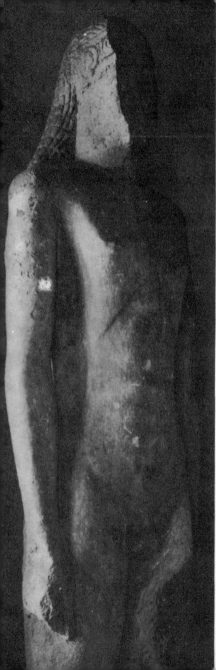

the monsters of the deep and fears the odor of the seals.[19] Water is certainly not the element on which his heart prefers to rest.

The fact remains, nonetheless, that the fifth Book is the first poem in known literature to describe the struggle of a man fallen into the sea with the waves and the reefs, and in a way to make us share his anguish. Does there exist another account comparable with Crusoe's shipwreck? Despite seven other storms which it recounts (a considerable number, in which we can see the convention for epics-to-come forming before our eyes) *The Odyssey,* for this single episode, deserves to be hailed as the first poetic expression of the victory of man over the blind element. Here, we must make one correction: of man assisted by the gods – for Ulysses, to maintain himself for two days and two nights upon the waves, has rolled himself in the mantle of Ino, the White Goddess.

The poet and the sea: here we are brought back to the search for his key images. We are given much less assistance than in *The Iliad,* with its abundance of comparisons. *The Odyssey* contains approximately one-fifth

Ancient kouros from Thebes

as many; [20] and, though it is noticeably shorter, this disparity remains striking, even on ordinary reading. If we should insist on the same author for both epics, we might argue that the subject of *The Odyssey* is less likely to require comparisons. Still, even if we accord them merely the value of "embellishments" designed to ornament a narrative overcrowded with violent emotions, there would be no lack of episodes which would provoke them in greater numbers if the poet "imaged" as he breathed. As a matter of fact, he happens – accidentally – to cultivate "ornament" out of simple respect for an acquired technique. Never would a connoisseur of wild beasts like the Master of *The Iliad* have imagined a doe sheltering her fauns in a lion's cave! The man who fabricates this false "ornament" has never sniffed a jackal's den, a fox's earth.

The lines of investigation must be multiplied to reach the peaks that dominate the author's inner landscape. On one of them, we have already discovered the many idols of the Mother. Another has thrown us upon the mountainous waves. We must now procede by looking back to *The Iliad*: its solitary contemplator is missing here. And with him disappears the architecture of clouds, of peaks and of gulfs. A rocky mountain is merely a projectile in the hands of the Cyclops, himself compared to a peak. Enormous as we may make him (and after all he has to fit into his cave), this is a remarkable downgrading inflicted upon the mountains! And there is no escape into the clouds, despite a description of Olympus, given in Book VI, worth quoting here:

On these words, the owl flew off, Pensive Athena,[21]
Towards Olympus, where the gods are said to live
Unshaken forever. Neither winds nor rain beat upon it,
Nor does the snow ever come near, but the clear sky
Spreads cloudless above it; and a white radiance floats about it.

The bard has stronger affinities with the earth. Here are his three caverns: that of Calypso, that of the Cyclops, and that, less famous, on the shores of Ithaca, which serves Ulysses as a hiding place for the Phaeacian gifts. The second is a *donnée* of folklore; it is, in its remote origins, an initiation grotto. The poet has not invented it, but he has delighted in describing it, combining effects of firelight and shadow, equipping it as a stable and a dairy. The other two have also awakened him from his dreams; they have a complete ex-

147

istence, clearly dream-derived, in the Cyclopean nightmare; the third cavern interprets groups of stalactites as magical phenomena. On each occasion the poet's soul has responded to the suggestion of this "archetype." Besides, he had only to listen to his Aegean subconscious, accustomed as it was to sacred grottoes.

From the cavern on Ithaca, temporary depot of precious objects, we shift by a sort of natural progress to the chambers that are used as a treasury, just as in dreams one image melts into another. We knew best of all Ulysses' treasury, which is also the armory, and plays on this account an important part in the final slaughter. But we also glimpse those of Alcinous and Menelaus. It is curious that Penelope's gesture of thrusting

The blinding of Polyphemus (Bibliothèque Nationale, Paris)

the key into the lock when she goes to the treasury for her husband's bow should be expressed by the same words, *aiming straight in front of her*, which, later on, are applied to Ulysses when he aims at the slender target formed by the holes of the twelve axes lined up one before the other. If there is a sexual symbolism in the bowman's exploit, the bard must have been unconscious of it (he has not invented the trial by archery, an old kingly rite); but, instinctively, he has doubled it with a parallel symbol, bearing witness to this symmetry by slipping into a useless formula (for one does not "aim" at a keyhole one is used to).

What are we to make of these images of treasure? Certainly in both epics the chief characters take pleasure in displaying their precious arms or their services of gold and silver; an affirmation of prestige more than a mercantile love of gold. Furthermore, these are immobilized and non-productive riches. In these ancient societies anterior to the use of money, the rich man acquires and hoards; he does not capitalize in this form (his active capital is in men and cattle). But in *The Odyssey*, the bard enjoys counting the gifts his heroes receive. If Ulysses invents false adventures, he does not fail to collect many gifts. The way he worries about those he has actually brought back, the satisfied eye with which he gauges those the suitors finally decide to bring Penelope, these are further indications. But there is still a better one: Athena has helped him arrange what he brought back from Phaeacia in the cavern on the beach; and, a little later, when he locks up in his treasury the weapons littering the great hall, it is Athena again who lights his way with a gold lamp. The Virgin is the patroness of her blessings.

We cannot draw ambitious inferences from the detail of the Odyssean landscapes, composed for the most part by juxtapositions of formulas. At least we can note, in contrast to the shadowy caverns, the frequency of cheerful compositions: groves around springs, orchards, flowery meadows. One of the great gods stops to contemplate the vicinity of the cavern where Calypso lives, as Ulysses stops before the garden and the palace of Alcinous. The attraction of calm water, of wet grass – which a man appreciates when he is used to rocky islands and parching summers, but to which he could not have responded in this prolonged and silent halt. He loves the earth, but not for its smile. A plain where the wind blows the dry

149

thistles, a commonplace summer scene on certain Mediterranean shores, is associated for him with the storm that carries off a wreck. Like the French classical writers, he prefers to the wild immensities "the shadow and the cool" of gardens, the landscape created by man.

One further characteristic which helps define the poet's imagination: he is sensitive to craftsmanship. The gesture of Ulysses turning his bow over and over in his hands at the moment he is about to try it is that of a good workman pleased with the feel of his tool. It is marvelously adapted to the situation, and gives the narrative a particular savor of something really seen. But a poet gifted in other ways would not have thought of it. In *The Iliad*, Homer has a long description of Pandarus drawing his bow (on the field of battle, but quite leisurely); he has not hit upon such a detail, nor has he a half-line to suggest any concrete aspect of the labor of the Achaean army building a rampart around its ships. In *The Odyssey*, on the other hand, he never fails to furnish details as to the construction of Ulysses' raft: everything is accounted for, from the tools used and the nature of the wood down to the way the beams are laid. Even if this particular kind of construction were furnished by some previous model, the insistence of the whole passage remains quite characteristic. In *The Iliad*, only a blacksmith god assisted by extraordinary robots seems to have deserved a close interest in his work; but the latter is as miraculous in its means as in its results. The poet has not intended to furnish a scene of artisan life; he has illustrated, according to the principles of the epic, the great actions of Hephaistos. In *The Odyssey*, the hero's hands are not defined as "man-killing." Of course they perform their murderous tasks energetically, but they turn with the same perfection to tasks which a shipmaster and a great farmer must know how to perform. The hand on the cithara is not ignorant of the hand on the plow; the Homer of *The Odyssey* has his hands on both.

From humor to fantasy

Thus from various points of view we can gradually make out a few temperamental characteristics. Above all, Homer loves to tell stories. They form of their own accord in his mouth. And this very work, "stories," with all that it implies of the popular, of the impromptu, of the spontaneous, even of the badly organized, suggests that such a poet is rather far from the true epic spirit. The heroic epic is the sister of History – and of the Legend of the Gods. *The Odyssey,* on the contrary, leads to a time when the minor divinities become fairies with wands, when monsters who are the sons of gods turn into ogres.

The bard, with his preference for fields (in this we may amuse ourselves by recognizing, already, the penchants of a city-dweller), for manual labor, for the conviviality of feasts, with his love of dogs (the consolation of a man too fond of *the eternal woman* ever to be satisfied by women), easily assumes a "petty-bourgeois" aspect which hardly seems encouraging to the writing of a poem in which fantasy assumes such importance. But we must be careful. This man allows within himself the bubbling of dreams originating in our deepest subterranean sources. Perhaps a little in spite of himself. Yet they pour forth. But does he know their worth?

ΟΛΥΣΕΥΣ   ΒΟΡΙΑΣ

There was a time when scholars enjoyed talking about his naivety. Actually, we are never quite sure where obedience to a certain inner youthfulness of spirit (which makes him accept his "fairy tales") leaves off and where a kind of humor, of which he has elsewhere given definite proof, begins. We cannot mistake his intentions when he takes the listener into his confidence. For instance when Ulysses, landing by night on the shores of Ithaca, cannot – when day comes, and with it fog – recognize the country so long yearned for. A young shepherd appears, but the poet warns us it is really Athena. And Ulysses, without suspecting it is she, but because he suspects all men, immediately begins inventing a story to explain his presence. We know that this man, wily as he is, is about to make a fool of himself; we watch him sink deeper and deeper in his mistakes: what a pleasure to see the trickster tricked! A device whose effect is so sure that stage comedy has only to take it over entire. A little later, the business is still more pointed: before Eumaeus, to whom he has not revealed himself, Ulysses describes himself in action beneath the walls of Troy, during a night on patrol. Not only does he use the guise of an admiring witness to brag up his own skill, but he lets it be understood, doing so, that he needs a blanket and, without having to ask for it, is given one. At the same time, the bard manages to make fun of the heroic epic, which is reduced to a tale told by a frostbitten watchman. We must be on our guard with a man who serves out his humor so astutely.

153

It also becomes extremely hard to say whether the adventure in the Cyclops' cave is equally moving to him at every point. The description of Polyphemus' first meal, with its violent details – men felled to the ground, their brains dribbling out, their bodies torn limb from limb, the bones themselves devoured – may well be an ingenious effort to terrify us. Or is it the slightly sadistic sport of a civilized man who laughs up his sleeve if we show how horrified we are? And what about the six sailors in Scylla's tentacles when they wave their arms and legs in the air, calling their leader to the rescue? Is this realism or caricature? We can be sure that legends never indulge in such details – in folklore, one is felled without phrases.

If the bard had had a passion for really profound fantasy, would he have consented to sacrifice such promising episodes as the Lotus-eaters, the Lestrygonians, the Sirens, or Aeolus? I doubt it. He knows how to break the tension of even the most dramatic events: the island of goats is juxtaposed to the cave of the Cyclops: the moving moment in the Circe episode is sandwiched between a lucky hunt and a whole winter of good weather. So he could have remained faithful to his principle of alternating emotions without so many sacrifices.

Which does not keep us from recognizing – in a certain sustained tone of voice or in certain emphases – those moments

Corè (Persephone) from Athens

when the narrator is caught up in his own invention. The arrangement of the poem is enough to show the interest he feels in the Journey to the land of the Dead. This episode forms the center of Ulysses' navigations: around it are disposed in equal number the other stages of his journey, indicated by curious symmetries. It is possible that the poet has seen in the confrontation of his hero [22] and the Shades a decisive means of putting in the shade the adventures of the Argonauts, whose celebrity he himself attests; we can understand still better that, in this case, he has given this section particular care.

His art puts several emotional elements into action. Even before the departure of the seafarers, he plays with a mythical geography charged with terrors: Ocean, the limit of the world, which must be crossed; the infernal rivers, particularly Pyriphlegethon, whose etymology evokes the images of fire and conflagration, and the Styx, feared by the gods themselves; Persephone's sacred wood (tall black poplars and willows which, by their malignant influence, *destroy the fruits of the earth*); [23] and Erebus, that is, the Shadow. He does not describe the landscape more concretely: what would be the use? No one

To escape Polyphemus .

could have seen it; the Achaeans, skirting the country of the Cimmerians, have reached a land of "mist and clouds" where the sun's rays never penetrate. This obscurity can only deepen as they advance toward the realm of Hades (though it is not subterranean); the Shades can only be discerned and recognized when they approach. But what moves the bard most deeply and touches his listeners most directly is the human pathos: the conversation between Ulysses and his mother, his futile efforts to embrace her phantom, the complaint of Achilles degraded by a dishonorable survival, the final panic before the crowds of Shades. And such anguish, such dread are only all the stronger for being expressed in such solemn places, with their fearful and execrated names, in the shadows cast by the vault of the sky, a vault of bronze, where it joins the edges of the terrestrial disc.

But that Homer was himself aware of the pathos of darkness, and affected by it, is further proved, beyond the darkness of the cavern which the Cyclops dissipates in a sudden gleam of light from his fire, by the supernatural shadows which only the soothsayer Theoclymenes sees around the suitors at table, enveloping a cortege of Shades already bound for Erebus.[24] Much more than fabricated dreams all too easy to interpret which occasionally occur in the narrative, this vision deserves to be called prophetic.

Homer thus possesses an imagination sufficiently diverse to incline sometimes toward unreal adventure, sometimes to risk a knowing smile with the skeptical reader, sometimes to provoke great tragic sentiments, sometimes to describe, lovingly, our most banal activities. Is there another epic in which we watch the servant girls begin the morning housework? Yet it is they who, the evening of that same day, will scrub the same *megaron* (the great central hall) now full of corpses and blood. This contrast, which the bard has been discreet enough not to accentuate, is not a theatrical effect; it originates quite innocently in the narrator's inmost nature.

Ulysses' Island, at Corfu.

What authors and when?

If an increasing number of "Homerists" are rallying to the idea that *The Iliad* and *The Odyssey* are not by the same author, it is not for any historical or linguistic reasons. All that the study of the language reveals, all that the allusions to the contemporary *milieux* of both epics (to the delicate degree that they can be separated from poetic description of a remote heroic period) demand, is that several decades occur between the older *Iliad* and the younger *Odyssey*. Since we cannot date them with any precision, and since, moreover, we can easily be mistaken as to the time necessary for the evolution of the language, nothing in principle actually contradicts the possibility, as long as we are occupied with such considerations, that the same man composed *The Iliad* at about thirty and *The Odyssey* after sixty. And when we think that the same author could write *Hermann und Dorothea* on the one hand, and *Faust* on the other, or again the *Odes et Ballades* and then *La Légende des Siècles*, it is easy to explain stylistic differences by the differences in subject and by the evolution of the personality under the effects of age. About which, as about the dates, we can argue indefinitely, to the delight of the scholars.

It remains to be seen if these disputes penetrate to the sources of the poetic imagination. It is in this area that the philological tradition is too limited, so that we must complete it by a flexible use of "depth psychology." The term may seem ambitious, even somewhat absurd: yet it has the advantage of keeping that all too easy word "subconscious" out of the spotlight. Such a word is all the less satisfactory, in relation to poetic work, since the brilliant quality of certain solutions necessitates, on the contrary, the idea of a "supraconscious," at the same time that the methodical use the poet makes of them supposes a superior lucidity which is relaxed as seldom as possible. The term is unimportant; the analysis of images which haunt the nights and the reveries of a poet is no less precious a guide in the determination of his profound inclinations.

There can be no question, in the space of a few pages, of basing an exhaustive study of this kind on texts so extensive and so guarded by the use of traditional formulas. It seems, however, that the soundings already performed suffice to reach two imaginative levels too different by nature to coexist in the same man.

As for the sensory faculties, their continuous exercise in poetic work can only refine them and make them penetrate deeper into the objects to which they are applied; thus Victor Hugo's eye pierces gradually beneath exterior lights and shadows to a vision of things from within, animated with blacks more secret, and flashes of light more spiritual. How account for the fact that the Homer of *The Iliad*, in writing *The Odyssey*, should have ceased to rule over landscape with that eagle eye of his? In such cases, we cannot speak of the requirements of the subject matter: once you have it, you do not lose your eye. Even a blind man, if he has seen the world in his youth, continues to transcribe it with the sensitivity once peculiar to his own retina.

Consequently, two authors. This is at least a useful working hypothesis. In itself, it is no more questionable just because few classical authors happened to entertain it. They approached Homer with a virtually religious respect, but without knowing anything exact about him and without being able to ask themselves the questions which happen to preoccupy us. Their opinion merely proves this: At the moment when both epics crossed the Aegean to spread through all Greece, they were already united under the name of Homer. If we admit (and it is not much to ask) that they emerged from the same "studio," from a brotherhood of reciters associated on a family basis, of which the historically known Homerides of Chios provide an example, we shall not be surprised that they both carry the "trade mark" which attests their quality. We can even, without romancing too much, advance the notion that one of the authors might have been the grandson of the other and, according to the Greek custom, have borne the same name.

We should like to be able at least to propose two dates for the poems, if not for their authors. We must not conceal the fact that our efforts in this regard are open to interminable questions which reveal their fragility. Various considerations which would lose all their value by being set forth briefly lead us to place the composition of *The Iliad* slightly after 750 B.C. (Paul Mazon's date, for instance). In this case, *The Odyssey* is to be located in the seventh century B.C. and we may hesitate between the first and the second quarter, without being able to arrive at a date much later than 640 B.C. It is good to remember

161

that we are dealing with works composed, in all likelihood, by episodes long tested in public recitations before finding the form we now know them to have, as well as their definitive arrangement in the work as a whole. We could therefore not

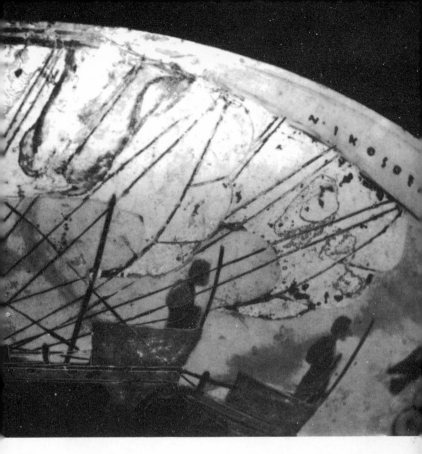

The Nicosthenes Cup (Louvre)

attribute any rigorous value to these dates of "composition."

Had we better assurances, they would not illuminate the texts much, and it is these and these alone which account for the spiritual humanity, with a voice which I think is still very much alive.

Man at grips with the sea

Poseidon has seen the raft of Ulysses approaching the country of the Phaeacians. Enraged that the gods should have let the hero escape in his absence, he raises the sea against him:

With this he drove the clouds into a heap and, trident in hand, tossed together the desolate waters. He summoned all the violent gusts that were in all the winds and let them loose, blind-folding sea and land with storm-clouds. Night leaped into heaven. Mightily the surge rolled up, for east wind clashed upon south wind, the ill-blowing west with the north wind from the upper sky.

Just as he ceased a huge rushing wave towered, toppled, and fell upon the raft, whirling it round. The winds came down confusedly in fierce turmoil and snapped the mast across in the middle. Yard and sail flew wide into the deep. Odysseus let the steering oar jerk from his hand and was himself thrown far from the raft into the body of the wave, whose weight of water long time buried him: nor did his struggles easily avail to get him out from under its wash, because of the hampering heavy clothes of honour in which divine Calypso had dressed him.

Yet at the last he did emerge, spewing bitter brine from his lips while other wet streams ran gurgling down his face. Yet not even in such dire distress did he forget his raft, but swam hard after it and caught it amongst the breaking waves and crouched down in its centre to escape, for the moment, the imminence of death.

His refuge was tossing hither and thither in the eddies of the waves, as when in autumn's stormy days the North wind pitches dried thistles along the fields, so that they lock spines into each other as they roll. Just in this way did the winds bowl the raft hither and thither across the face of the water. Sometimes the South wind flung it across to the North wind to carry, or the East wind would let the West wind chase it back.

The Odyssey, v

The White Goddess, Ino, gives Ulysses the veil from her hair to sustain him on the waves. But the hero, suspicious, hesitates to throw himself into the sea:

While his judgement and instinct pondered thus Poseidon the earth-shaker heaped up against him a wave of waves, a terror and tribulation, so high and combing it was. With this he smote him. It flung the long baulks of the raft apart as a powerful wind lays hold on a heap of dried chaff and whirls its straws everyway in confusion. Odysseus leaped astride a single beam, riding it as a man rides a plunging horse: while he tore off the clothes which had been fair Calypso's gift. Then he wrapped the veil about his breast and headlong leaped into the waves, striking out with his hands and urgently swimming.

The Odyssey, v

After two days and two nights drifting, at the third dawn, he joyfully sights land:

But when it was no further distant than the carry of a good shout, he could hear the heavy boom of surf against a broken shore and see how the great billows thundered down upon the naked coast in terrible clouds of spray which spattered all the sea with salty foam: for here were no inlets to welcome ships, nor roadsteads: but tall headlands, crags and cliffs. Then did the knee-joints and courage ·of Odysseus fail him, and sadly he questioned his own brave spirit: –

"Woe is me! Has Zeus let me behold this land only to make me despair? See, I have won my way from the depths of the tide, to find that here is no escape out of the foaming waters. There face me walls of sheer cliff, about which tumultuous seas clash loudly; and smooth the rocks run up, steep-to, so that nowhere is there lodging for my feet to bear me free from disaster. Should I try to climb, the next wave would take me and fling me against the broken rocks; and my effort have been in vain. As for swimming further, on the chance of gaining some sheltered beach or quiet inlet of the sea, then there is fear that a fresh storm-blast may drive my groaning body again far into the fish-haunted deep: or some god may rear up against me leviathan from the sea."

The Odyssey, v

First cast upon a rock, he finally reaches the mouth of a stream where the god is at last moved by his prayer:

And the god forthwith allayed the current, smoothed out the eddies and made his way calm, safe-guiding him within the river's mouths. Odysseus' knees gave way together, and his sinewy arms: for his reserve of manhood had been used up in the long fight with the salt sea. The flesh had puffed out over all his body and the sea water gushed in streams from his nostrils and mouth. Wherefore he fell helpless, not able to breathe or speak, and terrible was the weariness which possessed him.

The Odyssey, v

Man's condition after death

Ulysses among the shades.

At length we were at the shore where lay the ship. Promptly we launched her into the divine sea, stepped the mast, made sail and went: not forgetting the sheep, though our hearts were very low and big tears rained down from our eyes. Behind the dark-prowed vessel came a favourable wind, our welcomed way-fellow, whom we owed to Circe, the kind-spoken yet awesome Goddess: so when each man had done his duty by the ship we could sit and watch the wind and the helmsman lead us forward, day-long going steadily across the deep, our sails cracking full, till sundown and its darkness covered the sea's illimitable ways. We had attained Earth's verge and its girdling river of Ocean, where are the cloud-wrapped and misty confines of the Cimmerian men. For them no flashing Sun-God shines down a living light, not in the morning when he climbs through the starry sky, nor yet at day's end when he rolls down from heaven behind the land. Instead an endless deathful night is spread over its melancholy people.

We beached the ship on that shore and put off our sheep. With them we made our way up the strand of Ocean till we came to the spot which Circe had described. There Perimedes and Eury-lochus held the victims while I drew the keen blade from my hip, to hollow that trench of a cubit square and a cubit deep. About it I poured the drink-offerings to the congregation of the dead, a honey-and-milk draught first, sweet wine next, with water last of all: and I made a heave-offering of our glistening barley.

After I had been thus instant in prayer to the populations of the grave I took the two sheep and beheaded them across my pit in such manner that the livid blood drained into it. Then from out of Erebus they flocked to me, the dead spirits of those who had died. Brides came and lads; old men and men of sad experience; tender girls aching from their first agony; and many fighting men showing the stabbed wounds of brazen spears – war-victims, still in their blooded arms. All thronged to the trench and ranged restlessly this side of it and that with an eerie wailing. Pale fear gripped me.

The Odyssey, xi

Ulysses speaks with the various shades, including his mother, whom he tries to embrace:

While my heart pondered the word a longing rose in me to take in my arms this spirit of my mother, though she were dead.

Thrice I stepped toward her for an embrace, and thrice she slipped through my grasp like a shadow or a dream. The pain conceived in my heart grew very bitter.

The Odyssey, xi

He also sees Achilles, who reveals his scorn for the condition of the Shades:

"How I envy your lot, Achilles, happiest of men who have been or will be! In your day all we Argives adored you with a God's honours: and now down here I find you a Prince among the dead. To you, Achilles, death can be no grief at all." He took me up and said, "Do not make light of Death before me, O shining Odysseus. Would that I were on earth a menial, bound to some insubstantial man who must pinch and scrape to keep alive! Life so were better than King of Kings among these dead men who have had their day and died."

The Odyssey, xi

The Elysian Fields promised to Menelaus:

"Hear lastly the fate decreed you, O Menelaus, cherished of Zeus. You are not to die in Argos of the fair horse-pastures, not there to encounter death: rather will the Deathless Ones carry you to the Elysian plain, the place beyond the world, where is fair-haired Rhadamanthus and where the lines of life run smoothest for mortal men. In that land there is no snowfall, nor much winter, nor any storm of rain: but from the river of earth the west wind ever sings soft and thrillingly to re-animate the souls of men."

The Odyssey, iv

Queens and goddesses

Before Telemachus and Menelaus, Helen appears, in her palace in Lacedaemonia:

Helen, like a vision of Artemis of the golden distaff, came out from her high-coffered, incense-laden room with her women; of whom Adraste carried the graceful reclining-chair for her mistress while Alcippe had her soft woollen carpet and Phylo a silver basket given the queen by Alcandre, wife of Polybus, a dweller in Egyptian Thebes, that richest in palaces of all the cities of the earth. Polybus himself had given to Menelaus two bathing-tubs

of silver and a pair of three-legged cauldrons and ten talents in gold: while his wife added for Helen other wonderful gifts, such as a spindle all of gold, beside this silver basket which the maid Phylo now brought in and set beside her. The basket was mounted on a wheeled carriage also of silver and the rims of it were carried out in gold. It was heaped full of the smoothest yarn and across it, at the moment, lay the distaff wound with wool of a wood-violet blue.

The queen sat down in her long chair which had a stool to support her feet.

The Odyssey, iv

Hermes seeks out Calypso on her island on behalf of the gods, to order her to let Ulysses go:

But when at last he attained that remote island, he quitted the purple sea and went inland as far as the great cave in which lived the nymph of the well-braided hair. He chanced to find her within where a great fire burned on its appointed hearth, perfuming the island far across with the fragrance of flaming cedar-wood logs and straight-grained incense trees. Inside the cavern the nymph's sweet voice could be heard singing as she went to and fro before her loom, weaving with a golden shuttle.

The Odyssey, v

Nausicaa explains to Ulysses that when he reaches the palace he must first turn to her mother, Arete:

But when the buildings and court have swallowed you up, then hurry your fastest through the great hall, till you find my mother. She will be sitting at the hearth in a glare of firelight spinning yarn tinctured with sea-purple, a marvel to the eye. Her chair will be backed against a pillar and her maidens all orderly behind her. My father's throne is propped beside hers, and on it he sits, drinking his wine and sitting like an immortal.

The Odyssey, vi

Scouts sent by Ulysses arrive at Circe's palace:

The party threaded the woodland glades till they found the hewn walls of Circe's house on a site which overlooked the country-side. Wolves from the hills and lions, victims of her witch's potions, roamed about it.

From outside the house-gates they heard Circe, the Goddess with the comely braided hair, singing tunefully within by the great loom as she went to and fro, weaving with her shuttle such close imperishable fabric as is the wont of goddesses, some lively lustrous thing. Polites, a file-leader very near and dear to me, then said to the others: 'Shipmates, this voice at the loom, singing so heartily that the floor resounds again, is a female voice – either of a woman or a goddess. Let us give her a hail back.' They agreed and shouted loudly. She came at once, opening her doors to bid them in.

The Odyssey, x

The death of the faithful dog

Accompanied by Eumaeus, who has still not recognized him, Ulysses finally reaches the gates of his home:

As they talked a dog lying there lifted head and pricked his ears. This was Argos whom Odysseus had bred but never worked, because he left for Ilium too soon. On a time the young fellows used to take him out to course the wild goats, the deer, the hares: but now he lay derelict and masterless on the dung-heap before the gates, on the deep bed of mule-droppings and cow-dung which collected there till the serfs of Odysseus had time to carry it off for manuring his broad acres. So lay Argos the hound, all shivering with dog-ticks. Yet the instant Odysseus approached, the beast knew him. He thumped his tail and drooped his ears forward, but lacked power to drag himself ever so little towards his master. However Odysseus saw him out of the corner of his eye and brushed away a tear, which he covered by quickly saying to Eumaeus in an off-hand way:

"Strange, that they let such a hound lie on the dung-hill! What a beauty to look at! though of course I cannot tell if he has speed to match, or is merely one of those show-dogs men prize for their points." Eumaeus answered, "That is the hound of a man who died far from home. If only he could recover the fire and life that were his when Odysseus left for Troy, how your eyes would open at seeing such speed and power. Put him on the trail and no quarry ever escaped him, not even in the densest thickets, so keen he was of scent. Now he has fallen low, his master having perished abroad and the heartless women caring for him not at all. Slaves, when their master's control is loosed, do not even wish to work well. Ah, the day a man's enslaved, Zeus robs him of half his virtue!" With this word he plunged into the house, going straight along the hall amidst the suitors; but Argos the dog went down into the blackness of death, that moment he saw Odysseus again after twenty years.

The Odyssey, xvii

Master and servants

*Eumaeus, the swineherd, once sold as a child to Laertes, Ulysses'
father, speaks to Ulysses, whom he has not recognized:*

Said the excellent swineherd: "I will tell it you in detail. Laertes
lives: but prays ever and ever that Zeus will let the life flicker
from his limbs in the hall. So bitterly does he lament his missing
son and the long-proven wife whose death has been a main grief
to age him before his time. Know too that she herself fell on
death for grieving after her famous son. A tragic end hers was,
such as I would wish to no kindly neighbour who had entreated
me well. Despite her sorrow I was careful and glad to ask after
her while she lived: for I was brought up by her with tall long-
gowned Climene, her youngest daughter. Together we grew up,
the mother honouring me almost like her own child, until both
of us came to blissful adolescence. Then they parted with her
(for a high wedding-price) to a man of Same, while me my lady
clothed and shod fairly and put to work on the farm. Her love
toward me ever grew, and it is that which I now miss."

The Odyssey, XV

Irony: The Trojan War as seen by a corporal ... who is a great leader

*Ulysses, who has come to Eumaeus' house disguised as a beggar,
wants a blanket for the night. Instead of asking for it at once, he
tells the following story:*

"I wish I were young, with the enduring vigour that was mine
in the days when we imagined and took on a surprise raid against
Troy. Odysseus was one of our leaders: with him was Menelaus,
son of Atreus, and for third in command (by their arranging)
went myself. We worked our way round the city till we reached
its massive wall and there we lay by the swamp beneath the
citadel, our panoply weighing us down into the reeds and dense
brake. As we waited the night turned very foul. The north wind
came down and it froze hard. Then snow began to fall, chill and
dry like rime, while ice plated our shields. The others all wore
cloaks over their tunics and so slept well enough, hunched up
with their shields over their shoulders; but I had left my cloak
with my fellows before setting out, having been fool enough to
think I should never feel cold. So there I was with just a gay
jerkin and my shield. When the third part of the night had come
and the stars were going down I nudged with my elbow against
Odysseus who lay next me, and whispered to his attentive ear:

175

'Son of Laertes, surely I will not be counted long among the living, for this cold is more than I can bear without my cloak. Something possessed me to come out only in my vest and now there is no helping it.'

Even as I spoke a notion flashed into his mind, for he was in a class by himself when either scheming or fighting were in question. He hissed at me sharply: 'Be quiet, lest some other Achaean hear you.' With that he propped his head on his bent arm and said in a low carrying voice: 'Listen, friends. I fell asleep and God has sent me an important dream to show how much too far from the ships we have come. I would have someone bear warning to Agamemnon son of Atreus, the shepherd of the people, that he may move us reinforcements from the leaguer.' At his word Thoas son of Andraemon leaped up nimbly, flung aside his purple cloak and broke into a run for the ships, while I snuggled into his garment till Dawn shone from her golden throne."

The Odyssey, xiv

Restraint in triumph

After the slaughter of the suitors, Telemachus goes to find old Euryclea:

Up with you now, aged dame and supervisor of our house-women. Come hither. My father calls you for somewhat he has to say. Not a word could she launch in reply. She opened the doors of the stately hall and paced in (Telemachus ushering her) to where Odysseus stood in a slaver of blood and muck amidst the corpses of his victims, like some lion that has devoured an ox at grass and prowls forth, terrible to the eye, with gory breast and chaps. So was Odysseus bedabbled from his hands right down to his feet. She, when she saw the corpses and the pools of blood, knew how great was the achievement and opened her mouth to raise the woman's battle-wail: but Odysseus checked her excitement and stilled her with these trenchant words, "Rejoice within yourself, beldam, and quietly. Keep back that throbbing cry. To make very glad over men's deaths is not proper. These fell by doom of the Gods and through the wickedness themselves had wrought, in disregarding good and bad alike amongst their earthly visitors. To such infatuation they owe their ignominious death.

The Odyssey, xxii

Penelope's final discretion

She was going down as she spoke, her heart in a turmoil of debate whether to keep her distance while she examined her dear lord, or go straight up at once to kiss his head and clasp his hand. So when at length she came in across the stone threshold it was to take a seat in the fire-light facing Odysseus, but over against the further wall. He sat at the base of a tall pillar, waiting with drooping eyelids to hear his stately consort cry out when she caught sight of him. But she sat there in a long silence, with bewildered heart. One moment she would look and see him in his face; and the next moment fail to see him there, by reason of the foul rags he wore – till Telemachus named her in disapproval. "Mother mine," he cried, "unmotherly mother and cruel-hearted, how dare you hold aloof from father, instead of running to sit by his side and ply him with questions? No other woman could in cold blood keep herself apart, when her man got home after twenty years of toil and sorrow. Your heart remains harder than a stone."

But Penelope explained: "Child, my heart is dazed. I have no force to speak, or ask, or even stare upon his face. If this is Odysseus in truth and at last, then shall we soon know each other better than well by certain private signs between us two, hidden from the rest of the world." At which the glorious long-suffering Odysseus smiled.

The Odyssey, xxiii

NOTES

1 "Translator's Note" attached to the New York edition of his *Odyssey of Homer,* Oxford University Press, 1932. I should like to point out that Lawrence was an archeologist by early training, collaborating in the diggings at Karkemish.

2 In *The Iliad,* 243 people who die are named: they often have at least the pretense of a history. Cf. Bassett, *op. cit.* p. 93.

3 Even at the period of Salamino (480 B.C.) some Greeks were convinced that they had witnessed prodigies of divine origin; cf. Herodotus VII, 65, 84, 94.

4 I must refer the reader to my *Genèse de l'Odysée* pp. 436-438.

5 Cf. the entire first volume of the work cited above.

6 In the study of the Oriental "sources," Mme. Stella (*Poema di Ulisse,* already cited) has reached, simultaneously with me, and independently of my studies, results which in some part coincide with my own, and in some part complete them. Cf. her first section, Chap. ii and iii.

7 Two examples: the obscurity almost impossible to dissipate with regard to the land of the Lestrygonians; in the story of the Oxen of the Sun, the strange phenomenon of the roast meat moaning.

8 Toward the end of the last century, a man from Aneyza, in the heart of the Arabian Peninsula, said to Doughty: "We have a language to come to the aid of our friends and ourselves, and to deceive our enemies, and in truth in most cases lies are more valuable than the truth." (Charles M. Doughty, *Arabia Deserta,* p. 257 of the extracts published in the Penguin Books edition.) A North African proverb declares, it seems: "Only the fool and the child tell the truth."

9 Book XX.

10 *The Republic,* 617e, a proclamation addressed to the souls that are to be reincarnated, to urge them to choose wisely.

11 Book XIV.

12 Book XVII.

13 Book XX.

14 A line from Book IV: *Because you are the husband of Helen and in their eyes the son-in-law of Zeus,* is suspect of having been added to explain Menelaus' election. The epic never sets a human being in the lineage of the gods in this way.

15 In North Africa, especially among the rural populations, this almost paralyzing respect for the old is still to be found. It must be seen in order to understand the same phenomenon among the ancients. Is it

on this account that there is no trace, in Homer, of conflict between the generations?

16 Cf. the remarkable study by W. B. Stanford, *The Ulysses theme, a study in the adaptability of a traditional hero,* Oxford, 1954.

17 I am pleased to refer to *Ulysse ou l'Intelligence* by Gabriel Audisio (collection "Les Essais," XX, Paris, Gallimard, 1946).

18 Cf. *Genèse de l'Odyssée,* "Ulysses' raft and Egyptian Navigation," pp. 399-400.

19 If these remarks surprise some of my readers, I can only refer them to the work cited above, pp. 601-618, where I have given my proofs.

20 Severyns, *Homère,* Vol. III: The Artist, p. 153.

21 A free rendering of the well-known epithet *glaukopis.* The Homeric texts *never* refer to the color of eyes; only their brilliance or their shape concern the bards. This is a strong reason not to accept the translation 'gray-eyed" so widespread in our day. We must also refer to the parallel formula for Hera, *boopis,* which we cannot avoid translating, at least literally, "ox-eyed." Hence here too: "owl-eyed Athena." Why? To understand this, one merely has to have seen at close hand, and sympathetically, any owl but particularly one of the smaller species: nothing could be more graceful and more meditative; precisely suitable to a young divinity who incarnates intelligence. Compare, for this impression of beauty, the popular French term *chouette* and the Italian *civetta,* both *owl* and *coquette.*

22 In my book, already too frequently cited, I have given a table of these symmetries. One can even add that the episode cuts the poem into two groups of a comparable number of lines (not counting Book XXIV, generally suspect).

23 An unaccustomed translation, which is defended in the same work, p. 363.

24 The character of Theoclymenes is rather clumsily attached to the action; the hypercritics, in their dissections, have cut him from the poem. He clearly exists only as a function of this brief scene, presage of the imminent destruction which awaits the suitors. But this was a "ready-made scene" which the imaginative writer conceives before knowing how he will use it and to whom he will give it. Theoclymenes is connected, moreover, to the *saga* of Melampous, which may have been a contemporary theme of which Homer was fond.

181

ON THE CORRECT USE OF HOMER

As to what Homer was for the Hellenic consciousness, we have not said everything when we have pointed out that children have learned him by heart as long as there have been schools in Greece, or even better: that Hellenized Egyptian children still studied him on the eve of the Musulman conquest. Nor when we have proved, with figures to support the claim, that no other ancient author, by far, is so often represented in the Greek papyri which the same Egypt furnishes us. Nor when we have analyzed the commentaries of the ancient scholars and thinkers. * We need to have lived in the streets and fields, among ordinary Greek people, to know how many times a day they refer to him and in how many circumstances they seek a decisive example from the poems: "My child, Achilles at your age. . . ." – "Friend, in your position, Ulysses. . . ."

This is the use of an epic in the civilizations where the oral tradition predominates. I have come to understand what Homer has meant for the Greek of the *agora* and the porticoes in reading, from the pen of one of their countrymen, how, in our own day, the milk-sellers of Bombay, in the train taking them home from the market, marvel over the *Ramayana*, how the shopkeepers read it between customers, how it is interpreted while following funeral processions: "Everyone has to die, that's certainly the Truth. Even Dasaratha, the holy father of Sri Rama, died. He died of grief because his beloved son and heir had to go into exile. A promise made in another life to his wife forced the king's hand. You have to keep your promises." ** That is how one might have moralized over the death of Achilles. "From time to time it happens that there is someone who can no longer endure the sufferings of Sita, and he wipes away his tears. And then he sells some salt, some lentils and eggplants, and then he goes back to the *Ramayana*." This, we can be sure, is how tears were shed for Penelope, Andromache, or Hecuba, between two weighings of sardines. The Greeks have lived with Homer. This is much better than merely reading him.

I turn to India again for another kind of lesson. Sri Auro-

* Cf. the dissertation by the Abbé F. Buffière, *Les mythes d'Homère et la pensée grecque*, 1956.
** Raja Rao, "Climat de l'Inde," in *Cahiers du Sud*, no. 336 (August, 1956), pp. 205-208).

bindo, who was not only a celebrated yogi and thinker, but a poet familiar with the Greek classics as well as with nineteenth-century European lyric poetry, had so active an admiration for Homer that upon his death he left considerable fragments of a poem in English called *Ilion*, which he had conceived, in his youth, as a sequel to *The Iliad*. What sustenance could he who sought to provide what we might call a descent of the Spirit among us and thereby a new humanity sanctified in its flesh as well as its soul – what sustenance, then, could he find in Homer, poet of the *vital*? Yet a poetry which realizes its own order of perfection, whatever it may be, reaches beyond mere reality. A poetry of the vital "can perceive the physical form of the gods . . . and discover a divine quality in even the most earthly, the most material and exterior ways of men; of this sort, we have Homer." When we read him, he says further, "we feel ourselves raised to a semi-divine stature." Yes, it is through the flesh, the blood, the moral condition, by extending them to the limits where they overthrow themselves, that Homer achieves the incorruptible and imperishable being of the gods themselves. And man receives from their proximity, from their friendship, that enlargement and that light which the master of Pondicherry unceasingly loved in Homer.

For anyone who has understood, thanks to this same India, how naturally an intelligent and experienced polytheism can find a place in the same mind with a God who is essence and person; and with That which is beyond the person as beyond Being and non-Being, the Homeric gods have a "presence" different from the Ingres-style figures of the old Mythologies. But one can have no interest in the gods (or not realize that one is interested in them) and find delight in living Homer merely for the company of his people.

What a pleasure to leave clustered in their Cimmerian mists all these catalogue tyrants, these paste-pot arbiters, all these chillers of the intellect, these dyspeptics of consciousness, these paralytics of the heart, all these invalids upon whom the Gorgon has turned her eyes, still half-men, already half stones for the steps of Persephone! And suddenly, in the open air, in the sunlight, these real men, these real women, these young girls: passion, purity, rage, laughter, sobs; these people who *are*, who walk the paths of their *being*, until they enter *their* deaths, eyes wide, a divine flame over their heads. Around them a real world, not a spiderweb of relationships or a colored gossamer, but a breathing, even in the blood, the sea like a heaving breast, the light that is one and the same for gods and men alike. A world one can do battle with but which, after the struggle, one can lean upon for support. For it *holds*. I pity the man who cannot live with Homer!

And I pity the poet who cannot live with Homer! If he does not feel in the muscles of his own language the power of the sustained rhythm, against the sides of his mouth the living water of the speech welling up from the depths, then he will never gather within himself the hidden rhyme and rhythm of the universe. If your soul is in a desk drawer, that's where your poetry will be too. Homer recalls the poetic conscience to its duty to the heights. "There is no great poem" when one thinks on a level with the table-top, or under the table. Which is not to suggest rewriting *The Iliad* today (in poetry, the question is to make, not to *re*make) but to seek the creative energy in the cosmic currents, in the clouds which hide the gods. Lucky Homer, who ran no risk of mistaking cigarette smoke for the Milky Way!

I have not spoken of Homer as a fanatic. To live with Homer does not mean "with Homer alone." To mention only those pre-Christian periods whose dignity and reality are still to be discovered, I have gained much from the *Dhammapada*, from the *Bhagavad Gita*, and from the Taoist fathers. I often ask them what I cannot ask of Homer. But having come to them so late, by the fault of our "provincial" culture, I do not feel toward them, as toward Homer or the Psalmist, a childhood friendship, the beautiful friendship of Patroclus and Achilles, of David and Jonathan. It is the grace of this friendship I want to revive among those who, as children, at the age of generosity and enthusiasm, have already encountered Homer. To the others, particularly those who mistrust the ancients a little, doubtful of what they have to give, I say in confidence: "For over twenty-five years I have not stopped studying Homer. Yet each time I begin reading him again, I realize I do not know him yet. (And it shows, those more erudite than I will say!) Probably because I am slow-witted. And perhaps, too, because he can no more be exhausted than a true man: a man connected with the infinite. How many such men do you know?"

ACKNOWLEDGMENTS

We should like to thank the publishers of the following volumes, from which we have borrowed some of the photographs that illustrate this book:

Béquignon, *Paysages et images de l'Iliade* (Budé, 1945), pp. 18, 42, 43. – Wegner, *l'Art grec* (Massin, 1955) pp. 20, 39, 133, 134. – "Archeology," *Courrier de l'Unesco*, p. 24. – Matz, *Le monde égéen* (Buchet-Chastel), pp. 4, 6, 27, 184. – Wade Gery, *The Poet of the Iliad* (Cambridge, 1952), front cover, p. 36. – Lorimer, *Homer and the Monuments* (London, Macmillan, 1950), pp. 44, 114, 181, 184. – Jonkees and Verdenius, *Planetas bij Homerus*, pp. 48, 56, 58, 63, 64, 68, 72, 73, 79, 87, 124, 125, 144, 152, 153, 155, 156, 181. – Bonnard, *Civilisation grèque* (Clairefontaine), p. 75. – *Art Treasures of the British Museum* (Thames and Hudson Ltd., 1957) pp. 95, 98, 188, 189.

The illustrations on pages 166, 171, 174, 179 represent fragments found in the Aegean Sea, at present in the National Museum of Athens. On page 4, the clay tablet from Pylos, linear script B.

Seymour-Magnum: p. 8. British Museum: pp. 10, 11, 95, 98. Chris Marker (Éditions du Seuil): pp. 12/13, 15, 16, 29, 33, 46/47, 93, 116/117, 151, 154, 156, 182. Giraudon: pp. 31, 55, 60, 66, 81, 82, 110, 114, 122, 123, 128, 129, 137, 148. Archives photo: pp. 40, 141, 162, 190. Anderson-Viollet: pp. 50, 107. Boudot-Lamotte: pp. 84, 146, 158, 164, 166, 171, 174, 179. Alinar-Giraudon: pp. 70, 102. Viollon: p. 90. Fr. Brousseau: p. 118. Ainari-Viollet: pp. 2 and 3 of cover.

Coin from Ios, fourth century B.C.: Homer clearsighted

Blind Homers from Modena and Bonn